WOK COOKERY

compiled by Suzy Powling

CHANCELLOR
PRESS

CONTENTS

NOTES
Standard spoon measurements are used in all recipes:
1 tablespoon = one 15 ml spoon
1 teaspoon = one 5 ml spoon.
All spoon measures are level.

Ovens should be preheated to the specified temperature.

In all recipes quantities are given in both metric and imperial measures. Follow one set of measures only, as they are not interchangeable.

All microwave information in the recipes is based on a 650 watt oven.

Ingredients and garnishes marked with an asterisk are explained on pages 10–13.

First published in Great Britain in 1991

This edition published in 1993 by Chancellor Press
an imprint of Reed Consumer Books Limited
Michelin House, 81 Fulham Road, London SW3 6RB
and Auckland, Melbourne, Singapore and Toronto

Reprinted 1993 (four times)

Copyright © 1991 Reed International Books Limited

ISBN 1 85152 319 7

A CIP catalogue record for this book is available from the British Library

Printed in China

INTRODUCTION

While it is utterly simple in its design, the wok is also one of the world's most beautiful cooking implements because it fulfils its function so perfectly. An essential piece of equipment in the Oriental kitchen, the wok has many more uses than basic stir-frying, as the recipes in this book make clear.

What makes a wok distinctive is its shape. Traditionally a hemisphere, the wok was made in this way so that it would fit snugly into a bed of burning coals, giving perfectly distributed all-round heat. The rounded shape also ensures that stir-fried ingredients always return to the centre, however vigorously you agitate them. Modern versions either have a small flattened area on the bottom so that they can stand on a hob, or come with a separate round metal stand that keeps the wok in place over the source of heat. Cantonese woks have two small handles, one on each side, while pau woks have a single, long handle like a Western frying pan. Metal handles become very hot in use. When choosing a wok, look for one with handles with wooden grips.

The ideal material for a wok is carbon or tempered steel. This rather thin metal heats up quickly. While it is very responsive to changes in temperature, a quality that is particularly important to successful stir-frying, carbon steel maintains high temperatures well. Stainless steel and non-stick woks do not conduct heat as efficiently and the results will be inferior. Gas hobs are best for cooking with a wok, especially for stir-frying. Modern electric hobs are almost as good, but can only be used for flat-bottomed woks. Ceramic hobs are unsuitable.

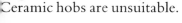

ACCESSORIES

A good wok is not an expensive item, but will prove to be an invaluable addition to your *batterie de cuisine*. With a few simple accessories, it becomes an unusually versatile instrument, giving you the opportunity to make not only delicious stir-fried dishes but also recipes based on techniques of steaming, braising and deep-frying. Many classic Chinese recipes call for 'cross-cooking' – that is, a combination of different techniques – which can all be performed in the wok.

A **stand** to support round-bottomed woks is essential, and is also necessary for flat-bottomed woks when deep-frying. For braising and steaming a **lid** is equally indispensable. The most practical choice is a stainless steel or aluminium lid, neither of which will rust. Make sure that the lid fits well and that it has a wooden knob or one which will not become too hot when in use. A **steaming rack** or **trivet** is also important for cooking in the wok. It is sometimes included as part of a wok kit, but can be bought separately.

Bamboo steamers are very useful because they can be rested in the wok and several layers can be stacked one on top of another to cook or reheat a selection of dishes at the same time. If you are going to buy a set, choose those with a reasonably large diameter.

A wok **rack**, which fits just inside the rim, is useful for deep frying in batches.

A long-handled **spatula** is the best instrument for stirring and tossing ingredients. Long **cooking chopsticks** are very efficient for stir-frying and it is more fun to use authentic cooking implements when preparing Oriental food. You will also need a **ladle**. For lifting foods that have been deep-fried, a **bamboo strainer** is ideal, but you can use a **slotted spoon**.

Preparing ingredients for stir-fried dishes means a good deal of chopping and slicing. For this good **knives** and a solid **chopping board** are indispensable. A **food processor** reduces preparation time to a minimum, but most Oriental cooks would not use it for cutting meat.

Care of the wok

A traditional carbon steel wok must be 'seasoned' before use. When new, it will be covered with a thin film of protective oil. Scrub off the oil with very hot soapy water or a cream cleanser using a scourer. Rinse thoroughly in very hot water and wipe dry. Place the wok over a low flame until it is hot and completely dry. Using a wad of kitchen paper, rub a little cooking oil over the entire surface of the wok. The paper will become black. Heat the wok again and rub over the surface a second time with a fresh wad of paper and more cooking oil. You may need to do this a third time before the paper comes away clean. The wok is now ready.

After cooking, wash the wok in very hot water only – do not

use soap – and dry it thoroughly, first with a tea towel and then by heating it over the flame. Rub over with a little cooking oil. Store your wok in the open, preferably hanging on a hook. If you do not use your wok very often, it may begin to go rusty, and you will have to repeat the original seasoning process.

COOKING TECHNIQUES

The wok is the original all-purpose cooking pot, and can be used to produce an astonishing variety of dishes using a number of techniques.

Stir-frying

Frying food quickly in a little oil is a cooking method not unknown in the West – the French technique of sautéing is a European approximation – but the art of stir-frying has become the most familiar and the most popular aspect of Oriental cookery. Stir-fried dishes are cooked at great speed, so that the ingredients retain their natural bright colours and fresh textures, as well as a high nutrient content. To health-conscious cooks and their families, flavourful stir-fried dishes are heaven-sent.

Ingredients for stir-fried dishes must be very carefully prepared so that they are all cooked and ready to serve at the same moment and because of the speed of cooking, everything must be cut up small to expose the maximum surface area to the heat. Chinese stir-fried dishes invariably look as good as they taste because the separate components are chosen for quality and freshness and prepared in order to contribute to a generally harmonious effect. Colour is an important element, but shape is another: when cutting up ingredients the Oriental cook will ensure that they are uniformly cut to look pleasing together and according to the cut of meat or type of fish or vegetable.

Vegetables are usually cut on the diagonal or shredded; meat is cut across the grain, often in thin strips. Placing the meat in the freezer for about 1 hour beforehand makes it easier to cut wafer-thin. It then defrosts almost immediately and is ready for cooking. You must use fresh meat when doing this and never refreeze meat that has already been frozen. Fish is usually cut into thin strips or cubed.

Always have everything to hand before you begin to cook. Put the main ingredients in little bowls in the order in which you will add them to the wok, with flavourings such as soy sauce, chopped garlic, grated ginger and salt and pepper near at hand. Once you have started to cook you should continue in a fast unbroken sequence until the dish is ready to serve. Always add the ingredients in the order specified in the recipe: this will ensure that each one is ready at the right moment. Heat the wok over the flame first; then add the oil. When it is smoking hot, reduce the heat slightly and place the first ingredient in the wok. Toss and turn the ingredients

7

rapidly, working from the centre to the sides of the wok with a spatula or cooking chopsticks. When adding a sauce or blended cornflour mixture, make a well in the centre of the ingredients then pour in the mixture and stir-fry vigorously over a high heat. If cornflour is used, make sure that the liquid boils for a thickened and glossy end result. Stir-fried dishes should be served as soon as possible after cooking.

The cooking oil flavoured in the East is groundnut or arachide oil, which is light, reaches high temperatures and does not imbue the food with a flavour of its own. Corn oil is good for fish; sunflower, rapeseed and safflower oils are high in polyunsaturates and give very good results in all recipes. Healthy though it is, olive oil is not recommended for stir-frying as it does not reach sufficiently high temperatures and has too distinctive a flavour. Sesame seed oil is not used in China for cooking, as it burns so easily, but is dribbled over cooked food as a finishing touch.

Shallow-frying
Shallow-frying differs from stir-frying in three ways: the amount of oil used is greater to start with, though a large proportion is subsequently poured off; the temperature is lower, and the cooking time longer. Larger pieces of food, such as fillets of sole, whole chicken breasts or escalopes of pork and veal can all be cooked in this way, usually with the addition of a simple sauce which has been cooked separately.

Deep-frying
The appeal of deep-fried food is its crispy outer texture, which is achieved by bringing the cooking oil to the correct high temperature and keeping it there while the ingredients are immersed. Because a wok is such a good conductor of heat, it is ideal for this process. Properly cooked in this way, food does not absorb fat because the crispy exterior – which may be formed by a batter – does not permit the oil to soak into it. When deep frying several small items, such as pancakes, dumplings, meatballs or cubed meat, do not put too many in the oil at once or the temperature will drop. Because of its shape a wok needs less oil than a conventional saucepan or deep-fat fryer: about 600 ml (1 pint) should be enough for most dishes. The recommendations about cooking oils given under stir-frying also apply to deep-frying.

As an alternative to batter, the traditional coating for deep-fried foods, there are a number of Chinese recipes in which ingredients such as small pieces of marinated chicken or fish are wrapped in paper parcels before being immersed in hot oil. The food is cooked by the all-round heat, without absorbing any oil at all. Diners unwrap their own parcels at the table.

For practical purposes, always use a wok stand on the cooker when deep-frying in a wok, and never leave a pan of hot oil unattended on the cooker.

Steaming

Steaming is one of the healthiest ways to cook because, unlike frying, it does not require any added fat and, unlike boiling, all nutrients are retained in the food itself rather than being leached into the cooking water. It is particularly successful with fish and vegetables, both of which keep their flavour and texture beautifully when steamed. This book also includes some delicious recipes for steamed chicken, duck and lamb. Because steaming is a relatively gentle form of cooking, only top quality cuts of meat are suitable, best sliced into small pieces before cooking. By contrast whole fish such as bass can be steamed with great success. The wok can also be used to steam couscous. While all steamed dishes can be cooked over boiling water, many are given an extra dimension by using a stock, court bouillon or other aromatic infusion instead.

Steaming is very widely used in Japan and is popular in all Oriental countries. There are two methods of steaming possible using a wok. The first involves placing the food on a plate (or a banana leaf, if you are in Thailand!) inside a bamboo steamer. Small portions of fish can be cooked in ramekin dishes or on scallop shells, loosely covered with foil. Some Oriental recipes call for small portions of food to be wrapped in a lotus leaf to retain moisture during cooking. Dolmades (page 49) is a classic Greek recipe cooked on the same principle. Put the lid on the steamer. Have the water ready boiling in the wok and set the steamer over it. Cover the wok tightly with a lid and leave for the recommended cooking time. In the second method the food, in a covered dish, is set on a rack or trivet in the wok. Whichever method is used, it may be necessary to top up with boiling liquid during the cooking time. Make sure that the liquid level in the wok does not touch the base of the steamer above. If it does, you will no longer be steaming but boiling, and the texture of the food will be mushy.

Remember that even when the flame is turned off underneath the wok, the boiling water or liquid remains very hot for some time and the food will go on cooking unless you remove it from the steamer straight away. Serve steamed food as soon as possible after it is cooked; if the food has to stand for some minutes, cover it with foil to keep warm.

Braising

In Chinese cooking braising is an example of cross-cooking, since food is first stir-fried over high heat, and then, after the addition of a little liquid, simmered at a lower temperature until tender. The wok must be covered with a lid for the second part of the cooking process. While the ingredients are prepared in the same way as for stir-frying, braising is not restricted to very tender cuts of meat only. The longer cooking time results in a nice blending of flavours, but braising is not well suited to any but the firmest types of fish.

HERBS, SPICES AND FLAVOURINGS

Even though the wok can be used for preparing dishes of all nationalities, you will almost certainly find that you use it to cook a number of dishes from China and other Asian countries. Many of these recipes include ethnic ingredients, the most common of which are described below. An increasing number of food stores and supermarkets now stock Oriental ingredients.

Asafoetida A pale yellow spice with a strong, distinctive flavour used in small quantities in some Indian dishes, particularly those including beans and lentils. It acts to enhance other flavours.

Cardamoms Highly aromatic white or green pods used in Indian cookery. Black or brown cardamoms are large, less aromatic and cheaper. Used whole, cardamoms should not be eaten: remove them from the dish before serving if you wish. If a recipe calls for cardamom seeds, carefully remove them from the pods rather than buy them ready packed – they will have lost a lot of their potency.

Clarified butter See ghee

Coriander leaves Fresh coriander leaves give a distinctive fragrant taste when added towards the end of dishes such as curries. They are widely used to garnish Indian, Chinese and Thai dishes. Flat-leaved parsley is as an approximate substitute.

Coriander seeds This important spice, used whole or ground in meat and vegetables dishes, is essential to curries. The flavour is faintly redolent of oranges.

Cumin seeds Both black and white cumin seeds are available. They are of central importance in Indian cooking. The flavour combines well with coriander seeds, green lentils and spinach.

Curry powder There is no single combination of spices that can claim to be 'true' curry powder. Those from India, Thailand and Malaysia vary in strength, and while some commercially prepared powders are very good, others are without merit. It is easy to make up your own, varying the ingredients to taste. See the recipe on page 12. Curry paste (see page 12) is useful for adding to stir-fried dishes.

Fennel seeds Fennel seeds have a hint of anise about them, and are an aid to digestion. They are particularly good with fish.

Fenugreek seeds Usually available in powder form, this is a powerful and bittersweet spice which is used sparingly in curries.

Fish sauce (nam pla) A very salty, thin, brown liquid made from shrimps, salt and soy. Widely used in South East Asian cookery. If you cannot obtain it, use anchovy essence.

Five-spice powder A Chinese seasoning. The components are star anise, fennel, cloves, cinnamon and Szechuan pepper.

Garam masala A blend of ground spices used in many savoury Indian dishes. It can be bought ready-made but can easily be made up at home from cardamom, coriander and cumin seeds with whole cloves and black peppercorns, lightly roasted and crushed.

Ghee Ghee is clarified butter and is the preferred frying medium for Indian dishes. It can be heated to a higher temperature than butter and most oils without burning. To make your own, melt 225 g (8 oz) unsalted butter over a low heat. Simmer until clear and a pale residue settles. Remove from the heat and spoon off any foam. Leave to cool slightly. Drain the clear oil from the top into a clean jar, pouring through a strainer lined with muslin. Cover. Makes 175 g (6 oz).

Hoisin sauce A thick, brown sauce with a hot, slightly sweet flavour, made from soya beans. Used in Chinese cookery to flavour stir-fried dishes and as a dip.

Mango powder Ground dried mangoes, which gives a sour flavour and golden-brown colour to Indian curries.

Mustard oil A yellow oil made from mustard seeds. It is pungent when raw but sweet when heated. Used in India for cooking vegetables and fish. Use groundnut oil as a substitute.

Mustard seeds Tiny round reddish-brown seeds used in Indian cookery. When fried in hot oil they become nutty in flavour.

Red bean paste A basic Chinese seasoning made from cooked soy beans, malt and salt. It is often used instead of soy sauce when a thicker, sweet sauce is required.

Saffron An expensive spice with a delicious flavour and glorious bright yellow colour. Used in India in rice dishes and puddings. Saffron threads are the stamens of a particular crocus. To use, infuse a few in a little hot water or milk for 10 minutes and add the liquid to the dish in preparation.

Szechuan peppercorns Although these little seeds look like pepper and have a slightly hot taste, they are not really peppercorns. Use as a condiment crushed with salt, or to flavour sauces.

Turmeric This spice is the ground root of a plant used in India to give a yellowish colour. Its flavour is much inferior to saffron.

MILD CURRY POWDER

This mixture will keep well for up to 18 months if stored in a large screwtop jar and kept in a cool dark place. Vary the quantities and ingredients to suit you own taste; more chilli powder will make a hotter mixture, for instance. Mix together:

GROUND SPICES	HEAPED TEASPOONS:
coriander	*12*
white cumin	*6*
gram flour (optional)	*5*
garlic powder	*5*
fenugreek seeds	*4*
with:	
paprika	*4*
turmeric	*4*
garam masala	*4*
curry leaves (optional)	*1*
asafoetida (optional)	*1*
ground ginger	*1*
mango powder (optional)	*1*
chilli powder	*1*
mustard powder	*1*
white pepper	*1*

Makes approximately 225 g (8 oz)

MILD CURRY PASTE

This paste will keep indefinitely as long as the liquid is evaporated during stir-frying.

225 g (8 oz) Mild Curry Powder
250 ml (8 fl oz) vinegar
250 ml (8 fl oz) sunflower oil

1. Mix the curry powder with the vinegar and enough water to make a paste which is not too runny.
2. Heat the oil in a large frying pan or wok. Add the paste: it will splutter at first but then subside. Stir-fry for 15–20 minutes until the water has completely evaporated to leave a creamy paste. The oil will rise to the surface when the paste is set aside. This means that the curry paste is fully cooked.
3. Transfer the slightly cooled paste to a warm sterilized bottle or jar. Heat a little more oil and pour it on top of the paste to act as a seal. Cover tightly with a lid.
Makes approximately 425 g (14 oz)

ACCOMPANIMENTS AND GARNISHES

Oriental food is famed for its visual appeal. Part of the art of presentation lies in using attractive garnishes as a finishing touch.

Spring onion flowers
Trim the spring onions and cut off the green part to leave about 7.5 cm (3 inches) total length. Cut halfway through the stalk lengthways 3 or 4 times. Place in iced water for 1 hour to open.

Tomato flowers
Use only firm tomatoes. Make zig-zag cuts around the middle with a small sharp knife, making sure the cuts go right to the centre. Carefully separate the 2 tomato halves.

Chilli flowers
Shred a chilli lengthways, leaving 1 cm ($^{1}/_{2}$ inch) attached at the stem end. Place in iced water about 1 hour to open.

MANDARIN PANCAKES

450 g (1 lb) plain flour, sifted
300 ml ($^{1}/_{2}$ pint) boiling water
1 teaspoon vegetable oil
a little sesame seed oil

1. Place the flour in a mixing bowl and gradually add the boiling water and vegetable oil, stirring all the time to make a firm dough.
2. Knead the dough into a roll 5 cm (2 inches) in diameter. Cut into 1 cm ($^{1}/_{2}$ inch) slices and form each piece into a small ball. Flatten each ball with the palm of the hand into a round flat disc.
3. Brush one side of each pancake with sesame seed oil and sandwich the pancakes together in pairs. Using a small rolling pin, roll each sandwich into a pancake 10–13 cm (4–5 inches) in diameter.
4. Heat a dry frying pan over a moderate heat. When hot, fry the 'sandwiches' one at a time, turning them as soon as air bubbles appear on the surface. Cook the other side until little brown spots appear underneath. Remove from the pan and peel the two layers apart gently.
5. Fold each pancake in half and place on a warmed serving dish, covered with foil to prevent them drying out.
Serves 4

SNACKS AND STARTERS

DEEP-FRIED DRUMSTICKS

2 tablespoons dry sherry
2 tablespoons soy sauce
pinch of sugar
4 cloves garlic, crushed
2 teaspoons finely chopped
    fresh root ginger
4 spring onions, chopped
8 chicken drumsticks
1–2 eggs, beaten
50 g (2 oz) plain flour,
    sifted
vegetable oil for deep-
    frying
TO GARNISH:
lemon slices
parsley sprigs

Place the sherry, soy sauce, sugar, garlic, ginger and spring onions in a bowl, add the chicken and turn to coat. Leave for 30 minutes. Remove the chicken; reserve the marinade.

Beat the egg into the flour. Gradually beat in the marinade. Dip the chicken into the batter and turn to coat. Heat the oil in a wok to 180–190°C/350–375°F, or until a cube of bread browns in 30 seconds. Deep-fry the chicken for 12–15 minutes, until golden brown and cooked through. Drain. Serve, garnished with lemon and parsley.
Serves 4

CRISPY PANCAKE ROLLS

250 g (8 oz) plain flour
pinch of salt
1 egg
300 ml (1/2 pint) water,
    approximately
vegetable oil for deep
    frying
FILLING:
1 tablespoon vegetable oil
1 teaspoon finely chopped
    fresh root ginger
2 cloves garlic, crushed
250 g (8 oz) boneless
    chicken breast, skinned
    and diced
2 tablespoons soy sauce
1 tablespoon dry sherry
125 g (4 oz) button
    mushrooms, sliced
2 celery sticks, chopped
3 spring onions, chopped
50 g (2 oz) peeled prawns
1 tablespoon chopped fresh
    coriander★

Sift the flour and salt into a bowl, add the egg and beat in sufficient water to give a smooth batter. Lightly oil a small frying pan and place over a moderate heat. Pour in batter to cover the base and cook until the underside is golden. Turn and cook the other side; repeat with the remaining batter.

To make the filling, heat the oil in a wok, add the ginger and garlic and cook for 30 seconds. Add the chicken and brown. Stir in the soy sauce and sherry, then the mushrooms, celery and spring onions. Increase the heat and cook for 1 minute, stirring. Remove from the heat, stir in the prawns and coriander and let cool.

Place filling in the centre of each pancake. Fold in the sides and form into a tight roll, sealing the edge with a little flour and water paste. Heat the oil in a wok to 180–190°C/350–375°F, or until a cube of bread browns in 30 seconds. Deep fry the rolls a few at a time for 2–3 minutes. Drain.
Serves 4

TEMPURA

vegetable oil for deep-frying
12 Pacific prawns, peeled
  but with tails left on
500 g (1 lb) plaice or sole
  fillets, skinned and cut
  into small pieces
8 button mushrooms
1 bunch spring onions, cut
  into 4 cm (1½ inch)
  lengths
1 red and 1 green pepper,
  cored, seeded and sliced
1 large onion, cut into
  wedges
½ small cauliflower,
  broken into florets
½ small aubergine, thinly
  sliced
BATTER:
1 egg
150 ml (¼ pt) water
125 g (4 oz) plain flour
50 g (2 oz) cornflour
pinch of salt
DIPPING SAUCE:
300 ml (½ pint) canned
  chicken consommé
4 tablespoons sweet
  vermouth or sherry
4 tablespoons light soy
  sauce

For the batter, lightly beat the egg in
a large bowl. Beat in the water until
frothy. Sift the flour, cornflour and
salt together and fold in gradually.
Place the oil in a wok and heat to
180–190°C/350–375°F, or until a
cube of bread browns in 30 seconds.
Dip the prawns, fish and vegetables
in the batter, then deep-fry in batches
for 2–3 minutes until golden. Drain
on kitchen paper; keep warm.

Heat the sauce ingredients
together, then pour into a warmed
serving bowl. Serve with the
Tempura.
Serves 4

CRISPY VEGETABLES

500 g (1 lb) mixed
  vegetables, e.g.
  cauliflower, beans,
  mushrooms,
  mangetout, peppers, cut
  into small pieces
vegetable oil for deep-
  frying
AVOCADO DIP:
1–2 cloves garlic, roughly
  chopped
1 shallot, roughly chopped
4 tomatoes, skinned,
  seeded and chopped
1 teaspoon chilli powder
2 avocado pears, peeled
  and stoned
1 tablespoon chopped fresh
  coriander★, if available
pinch of ground
  coriander★
1 tablespoon lime or
  lemon juice
BATTER:
125 g (4 oz) plain flour
pinch of salt
1 tablespoon vegetable oil
150 ml (¼ pint) water
2 egg whites, stiffly
  whisked

Place the dip ingredients in a food
processor or electric blender and
work until smooth. Spoon into a
serving dish, cover with clingfilm
and chill for not more than 30
minutes.

For the batter, sift the flour and salt
into a bowl, gradually beat in the oil
and water, then fold in the egg white.
Place the oil in a wok and heat to
180–190°C/350–375°F, or until a
cube of bread browns in 30 seconds.
Dip the vegetables into the batter,
then deep-fry in batches for 2–3
minutes, until golden. Drain on
kitchen paper. Serve with the
avocado dip.

Serves 4

17

VEGETABLE SAMOSA

125 g (4 oz) plain flour
$^1/_4$ teaspoon salt
25 g (1 oz) ghee★ or
    clarified butter
2–3 tablespoons water
oil for deep-frying
FILLING:
1 tablespoon vegetable oil
1 teaspoon mustard seeds★
1 small onion, minced
2 green chillies, minced
$^1/_4$ teaspoon turmeric★
1 teaspoon finely chopped
    fresh root ginger
salt
125 g (4 oz) frozen peas
125 g (4 oz) cooked
    potatoes, diced
$^1/_2$ tablespoon chopped
    fresh coriander★
1 tablespoon lemon juice

Make the pastry as for Meat Samosa
(below). Chill while preparing the
filling.

Heat the oil in a wok and add the
mustard seeds. Leave for a few
seconds until they start to pop, then
add the onion and stir-fry until
golden. Add the chillies, turmeric,
ginger, and salt to taste and stir-fry
for 3 minutes; if it starts sticking to
the pan add $^1/_2$ tablespoon water and
stir well. Add the peas, stir well and
cook for 2 minutes. Add the potatoes
and coriander, stir well and cook for 1
minute. Stir in the lemon juice. Cool
slightly.

Shape and cook as for Meat
Samosa. Serve hot or warm.
Serves 4

MEAT SAMOSA

125 g (4 oz) plain flour
$^1/_4$ teaspoon salt
25 g (1 oz) ghee★ or
    clarified butter
2–3 tablespoons cold water
vegetable oil for deep-
    frying
FILLING:
1 tablespoon vegetable oil
1 small onion, very finely
    chopped
1 clove garlic, crushed
250 g (8 oz) minced beef
$^1/_2$ teaspoon each ground
    coriander★ and chilli
    powder
1 green chilli, very finely
    chopped
1 tablespoon chopped fresh
    coriander★, if available
2 tomatoes, skinned,
    seeded and chopped
salt

Sift the flour and salt into a bowl.
Rub in the ghee or butter until the
mixture resembles breadcrumbs. Stir
in the water and knead until smooth.
Chill while preparing the filling.

Heat the oil in a wok and stir-fry
the onion and garlic for 5 minutes,
until golden. Add the beef and brown
quickly. Stir in the spices and cook
for 1 minute, stirring. Add the
chopped chilli and coriander,
tomatoes and salt to taste. Simmer for
20 minutes, then cool slightly.

Divide the pastry into 8, dust with
flour, roll out each piece into a thin
round, then cut in half. Fold each half
into a cone, dampen and seal the join.
Fill with a spoonful of filling, dampen
the top edges and seal. Heat the oil to
180–190°C/350–375°F, or until a
cube of bread browns in 30 seconds.
Deep-fry for 2–3 minutes.
Serves 4

COLOURFUL MUSSELS

2 kg (4 lb) mussels,
  scrubbed and beards
  removed
25 g (1 oz) butter
2 shallots, very finely
  chopped
3 cloves garlic, crushed
1 bulb fennel, very finely
  chopped
150 ml (¼ pint) white wine
1 tablespoon fennel leaves
1 tablespoon chopped fresh
  parsley
½ teaspoon chopped chives
1 carrot, cut into julienne
  strips
1 leek, trimmed, washed
  and cut into julienne
  strips
salt and pepper
50 g (2 oz) fromage frais
fennel leaves, to garnish

Discard any open mussels or those that do not shut when firmly tapped. Melt the butter in a wok. Gently stir-fry the shallot, garlic and fennel until cooked but not brown. Add the wine and simmer for 5 minutes. Put the mussels in the wok and sprinkle with the herbs and vegetable strips and season. Cover with a tightly fitting lid. Steam the mussels for 3–5 minutes, shaking the wok from time to time.

Discard any unopened shellfish. Transfer the mussels and vegetable strips to a warmed serving dish and keep hot. Blend the fennel and garlic mixture in a liquidizer, adding the fromage frais. Taste and adjust seasoning if necessary. Pour the sauce over the mussels and garnish with fennel leaves.
Serves 4

SQUID SALAD WITH CITRUS HERB DRESSING

750 g (1¹/₂ lb) prepared
   squid, sliced into thin
   rings
16 small green asparagus
   tips
75 g (3 oz) mangetout,
   topped and tailed
4 tablespoons lemon juice
salt
pepper
small head of radiccio,
   separated into leaves
   and washed
DRESSING:
4 tablespoons olive oil
3 tablespoons lemon
   vinegar
50 g (2 oz) fromage frais
   or quark
1 tablespoon chopped fresh
   herbs, e.g. dill, chervil,
   parsley

Lay a piece of wet greaseproof paper
in a bamboo steamer. Arrange the
asparagus, mangetout and squid on
top. Sprinkle over the lemon juice,
season well and cover. Place over a
wok of boiling water and steam for 3
minutes.

Meanwhile, mix all the dressing
ingredients in a screw–topped jar.
Season well. Arrange the radiccio
leaves on a small serving dish. Toss
the warm food in the dressing and
pile on to the radiccio leaves. Garnish
with sprigs of dill and chervil, if
liked.
Serves 4

CHICKEN CHAT

250 g (8 oz) boneless
  chicken breast, skinned
3–4 tablespoons lemon
  juice
2 tablespoons vegetable oil
1 onion, sliced
2 teaspoons Mild Curry
  Powder or Paste★
1 tablespoon tomato purée
4 small tomatoes, skinned
  and quartered
1 tablespoon vinegar
1 teaspoon dried mint
1 × 425 g (15 oz) can
  chick-peas, or 125 g
  (4 oz) dried chick-peas,
  soaked and cooked
1 tablespoon chopped fresh
  coriander, if available
salt
coriander sprigs to garnish
  (optional)
SPICES:
1 teaspoon white cumin
  seeds★
1 teaspoon black mustard
  seeds★
1/2 teaspoon fenugreek
  seeds★

Cut the chicken into 5 cm × 5 mm (2 × 1/4 inch) strips and rub with lemon juice. Leave to marinate for 1–2 hours.

Heat the oil in a wok and stir-fry the chicken for 5 minutes until it goes white. Remove the chicken and set aside.

Place the wok over a moderate heat and stir-fry the onion until soft and transparent. Add the spices and stir-fry for 1 minutes. Add the curry powder or paste, tomato purée, tomatoes, vinegar and enough water to prevent them sticking to the wok. Stir-fry for 3–5 minutes then add the mint, chicken, chick-peas and coriander. Season with salt. Cook until heated through. Garnish with coriander.

Serves 4
Note: freezing is recommended. See the note below Aloo Chat, opposite.

ALOO CHAT

500 g (1 lb) potatoes,
  peeled and diced
2 tablespoons vegetable or
  mustard oil ★
1 onion, sliced
2 teaspoons Mild Curry
  Powder ★ or Paste ★
1 tablespoon tomato purée
4 small tomatoes,
  quartered
1 tablespoon vinegar
1 teaspoon dried mint
1 tablespoon chopped fresh
  coriander ★, if available
salt

SPICES:

1 teaspoon white cumin
  seeds ★
1 teaspoon black mustard
  seeds ★
1/2 teaspoon fenugreek
  seeds ★

If you are using small new
potatoes, leave them
whole with the skins on.

Boil the potatoes until they are almost
cooked, strain and set aside. Heat the
oil in a wok and stir-fry the onion
until soft and transparent. Add the
spices and stir-fry for 1 minute. Add
the curry powder or paste, tomato
purée, tomatoes, vinegar and enough
water to prevent them from sticking
to the pan. Stir-fry for 3–5 minutes
then add the mint, potatoes and
coriander. Season with salt to taste.
Serve hot or cold, with a salad.

Serves 4

Note: freezing is recommended.
When cold, freeze in an earthenware
dish. This will keep for up to 3
months. Defrost at room temperature
for 6–8 hours to serve cold. To serve
hot, reheat in a covered dish in a
preheated moderate oven (180°C,
350°F, Gas Mark 4) for 45 minutes or
cover and microwave on Defrost for
20–25 minutes, stirring once, then
reheat on High Power for 8–10
minutes, stirring twice.

FISH AND SHELLFISH

SPICED PRAWNS IN COCONUT

4 tablespoons vegetable oil
1 large onion, sliced
4 cloves garlic, sliced
2 teaspoons ground
  coriander★
1 teaspoon turmeric★
1 teaspoon chilli powder
1/2 teaspoon ground ginger
1/2 teaspoon salt
pepper
2 tablespoons vinegar
200 m (7 fl oz) coconut
  milk
2 tablespoons tomato
  purée
500 g (1 lb) peeled prawns
TO GARNISH:
whole prawns in shell
lemon slices

Heat the oil in a wok, add the onion and garlic and stir-fry gently until soft and golden brown.

Mix the spices together in a bowl, add the salt and pepper, stir in the vinegar and mix to a paste. Add to the wok and stir-fry for 3 minutes, stirring constantly.

Stir in the coconut milk and tomato purée and simmer for 5 minutes.

Stir in the prawns and heat thoroughly for 2–3 minutes, until they are coated in the sauce.

Spoon into a warmed serving dish and garnish with whole prawns and lemon slices.
Serves 4

HADDOCK IN CHILLI SAUCE

4 tablespoons vegetable oil
2 large onions, sliced
3 cloves garlic, crushed
750 g (1 1/2 lb) haddock,
  fillets, cut into chunks
2 tablespoons plain flour
1 teaspoon turmeric★
4 green chillies (seeded if
  liked), thinly sliced
2 tablespoons lemon juice
175 ml (6 fl oz) thick
  coconut milk
salt
chilli flowers★, to garnish
  (optional)

Heat the oil in a wok, add the onions and stir-fry until soft and golden. Add the garlic and cook for 30 seconds. Remove the onions and garlic from the wok with a slotted spoon and set aside.

Toss the fish in the flour, add to the wok and brown quickly on all sides. Drain on kitchen paper.

Return the onions and garlic to the wok, stir in the turmeric and chillies and cook for 1 minute. Stir in the lemon juice, coconut milk and salt and simmer, uncovered, for 10 minutes, stirring until the sauce has thickened.

Return the fish to the wok and heat for 2–3 minutes. Spoon into a warmed serving dish and garnish with chilli flowers if using.
Serves 4

FILLETS OF SOLE WITH MUSHROOMS

500 g (1 lb) sole fillets,
  trimmed
1 egg white
2 tablespoons cornflour
vegetable oil for deep-
  frying
250 g (8 oz) button
  mushrooms, thinly
  sliced
2–3 spring onions, finely
  shredded
1 slice fresh root ginger,
  peeled and shredded
1 teaspoon salt
1 teaspoon sugar
1 tablespoon soy sauce
1 tablespoon Chinese rice
  wine, or dry sherry
125 ml (4 fl oz) fish or
  chicken stock
1 teaspoon sesame oil, to
  finish (optional)

This dish is not unlike the French *filets de sole bonne femme*. The fish can be skinned if preferred, but leaving the skin on helps to keep the fillets together.

If the fillets are very large, cut them in half. Put the fillets in a bowl with the egg white and cornflour. Mix together.

Heat the oil in a hot wok until fairly hot, then turn down the heat slightly. Deep-fry the fish until golden and crisp, stirring all the time with cooking chopsticks. Remove the fish from the wok and drain on kitchen paper.

Pour off all but 2 tablespoons of oil from the wok. Increase the heat to high and add the mushrooms, spring onions and ginger. Stir a few times and then add the salt, sugar, soy sauce, rice wine or sherry and the stock. Bring to the boil, return the fish to the wok and simmer for 2 minutes. Sprinkle over the sesame seed oil and serve.
Serves 3–4

SALMON WITH FENNEL

4 × 175 g (6 oz) fresh
  salmon steaks
6 tablespoons dry white
  vermouth
4 tablespoons dry white
  wine
pinch of dried mixed herbs
50 g (2 oz) butter
2 teaspoons finely chopped
  shallots
1 fennel bulb, thinly sliced
3 small leeks, thinly sliced
6 tablespoons double
  cream
1/4 teaspoon French
  mustard
salt and pepper
fennel leaves, to garnish

Place the salmon steaks in a flat-bottomed wok, pour over the vermouth and wine and add the herbs. Slowly bring to the boil, then cover and simmer very gently for 3–4 minutes. Using a slotted spoon, transfer the salmon to a warmed serving plate, cover with foil and keep hot. Rub the liquor through a sieve and set aside.

Wash the wok and return to the heat. Melt the butter, add the shallots, fennel and leeks and stir-fry for 4–5 minutes, without browning. Add the fish liquor, increase the heat and boil rapidly until it has reduced by just under half. Stir in the cream and mustard and season. Spoon the sauce over the salmon and serve immediately, garnished with the fennel leaves.

Serves 4

SOLE WITH SATE SAUCE

25 g (1 oz) butter
1 shallot, finely chopped
1 tablespoon each chopped
    chives, tarragon, parsley
grated rind of 1/2 lemon
8 Dover or lemon sole fillets
1 egg, beaten
4–5 tablespoons fresh
    breadcrumbs
vegetable oil for deep-frying
SATÉ SAUCE:
1 teaspoon each coriander★,
    cumin★ and fennel★
    seeds, lightly crushed
2 cloves garlic, crushed
125 g (4 oz) crunchy
    peanut butter
1 teaspoon dark soft
    brown sugar
2 green chillies, seeded
    and finely chopped
150 g (5 oz) creamed
    coconut, dissolved in
    450 ml (3/4 pint) hot water
3 tablespoons lemon or
    lime juice

First make the sauce. Heat the wok, add the crushed seeds and stir-fry for 2 minutes. Add the garlic, peanut butter, sugar, chillies and coconut milk, stir well and cook gently for 7–8 minutes. Stir in the lemon or lime juice; transfer the sauce to a bowl and keep warm. Clean the wok.

Melt the butter in a separate pan, add the shallot and cook for 1 minute. Stir in the herbs and lemon rind. Cool slightly, then spread the mixture over each fillet. Roll up each fillet, secure with wooden cocktail sticks, dip in the beaten egg, then coat in the breadcrumbs.

Heat the oil in the wok to 180–190°C/350–375°F, or until a cube of bread browns in 30 seconds. Deep-fry the fish rolls for 4–5 minutes, until golden. Drain on kitchen paper and arrange on a warmed serving dish. Serve with the Saté sauce.

Serves 4

MONKFISH IN HERB SAUCE

750 g (1 1/2 lb) monkfish,
    skinned
150 ml (1/4 pint) dry white
    wine
1 bouquet garni
salt and pepper
125 g (4 oz) butter
2–3 shallots, finely
    chopped
2 small leeks, finely sliced
2 tablespoons each freshly
    chopped parsley,
    thyme, watercress and
    marjoram
bunches of fresh herbs, to
    garnish

Place the monkfish in a wok, add the wine, bouquet garni and seasoning. Slowly bring to the boil, cover and simmer for 8–10 minutes, until the fish is tender. Remove from the heat and let cool. Lift the fish from the wok; drain and remove the bones.

Remove the bouquet garni, then boil the liquor rapidly until reduced by half. Pour off and reserve.

Melt the butter in the clean wok, add the shallots and leeks and stir-fry for 5 minutes, without browning. Stir in the chopped herbs.

Return the fish and reserved liquor to the wok and heat through gently. Season and serve garnished with herbs.

Serves 4

PRAWN BALLS WITH BROCCOLI

250 g (8 oz) uncooked
   Dublin Bay or Pacific
   prawns in shell
1 slice fresh root ginger,
   peeled and finely
   chopped
1 teaspoon medium or dry
   sherry
1 egg white
1 tablespoon cornflour
3 tablespoons vegetable oil
2 spring onions, finely
   chopped
250 g (8 oz) broccoli, cut
   into small pieces
1 teaspoon salt
1 teaspoon sugar

Wash the unshelled prawns, dry
thoroughly with kitchen paper, then
remove the black intestinal vein. Split
each prawn in half lengthways, then
cut into small pieces so that they
become like round balls when
cooked.

Put the prawn pieces in a bowl
with the ginger, sherry, egg white
and cornflour. Stir well, then leave to
marinate in the refrigerator for about
20 minutes.

Heat 1 tablespoon of the oil in a
wok, add the prawns and stir-fry
over moderate heat until they change
colour. Do not overcook, or they will
lose their delicate flavour. Remove
from the wok with a slotted spoon.

Heat the remaining oil in the wok,
add the spring onions and broccoli:
stir, then add the salt and sugar. Cook
until the broccoli is just tender, then
add the prawns and cook briefly,
stirring well. Serve hot.
Serves 4

BRAISED FISH WITH SPRING ONIONS AND GINGER

1 × 750 g (1¹/₂ lb) fish
(mullet, bream, etc)
head and tail left on
1 teaspoon salt
2 tablespoons flour
3 tablespoons vegetable oil
3–4 spring onions, cut
into 2.5 cm (1 inch)
lengths
2–3 slices fresh root
ginger, peeled and
shredded
SAUCE:
2 tablespoons soy sauce
2 tablespoons medium or
dry sherry
150 ml (¹/₄ pint) chicken
stock or water
1 teaspoon cornflour
pepper
TO GARNISH:
tomato halves
fresh coriander leaves★
cherries

Slash both sides of the fish diagonally with a sharp knife at 5 mm (¹/₄ inch) intervals as far as the bone. Rub the fish inside and out with the salt, then coat with the flour from head to tail.

Heat the oil in a wok until very hot. Lower the heat a little, add the fish and fry for about 2 minutes on each side or until golden and crisp, turning the fish carefully. Remove from the pan.

Mix the sauce ingredients together. Increase the heat and add the spring onions and ginger to the oil remaining in the wok. Stir-fry for a few seconds, stir in the sauce mixture and return the fish to the wok.

Simmer for a few minutes, then carefully transfer the fish to a warmed serving dish and pour over the sauce.

Garnish the dish with tomato halves, trimmed with coriander leaves and cherries. Serve hot.
Serves 3–4

STIR-FRIED SQUID WITH MIXED VEGETABLES

425 g (14 oz) prepared squid, cut into thin rings or slices
2 slices fresh root ginger, peeled and finely chopped
1 tablespoon rice wine or sherry
1 tablespoon cornflour
15 g (¹/₂ oz) dried Chinese mushrooms, soaked in warm water for 30 minutes
4 tablespoons vegetable oil
2 spring onions, cut into 2.5 cm (1 inch) lengths
250 g (8 oz) cauliflower or broccoli, divided into florets
2 medium carrots, cut into diamond-shaped chunks
1 teaspoon salt
1 teaspoon sugar
1 teaspon sesame oil

Place the squid in a bowl with half the ginger, the wine and cornflour. Mix well, and marinate for 20 minutes.

Meanwhile, drain the Chinese mushrooms and squeeze dry. Slice thinly, discarding the hard stalks.

Heat 2 tablespoons of the oil in a wok and add the spring onions and remaining ginger, then the cauliflower or broccoli, carrots and Chinese mushrooms. Stir-fry, then add the salt and sugar and continue cooking until the vegetables are tender, adding a little water if necessary. Remove the vegetables from the wok and drain.

Heat the remaining oil in the wok and stir-fry the squid for about 1 minute. Do not overcook the squid, or it will be tough and chewy. Return the vegetables to the wok, add the sesame oil and mix all the ingredients well together. Serve hot.

Serves 4

CRAB OMELETTE

2 spring onions
4 eggs, beaten
salt
3 tablespoons vegetable oil
2 slices fresh root ginger, peeled and shredded
175 g (6 oz) crab meat, fresh, frozen or canned
1 tablespoon rice wine or sherry
1 tablespoon soy sauce
2 teaspoons sugar
TO GARNISH:
shredded lettuce
tomato flower★
grape (optional)

Cut the white part of the spring onions into 2.5 cm (1 inch) lengths. Chop the green part finely and beat into the eggs, with salt to taste.

Heat the oil in a wok and add the white part of the spring onions and the ginger, then the crab and wine. Stir-fry for a few seconds, then add the soy sauce and sugar.

Lower the heat, pour in the egg mixture and cook for a further 30 seconds.

Transfer to a warmed serving plate and garnish with shredded lettuce. To finish, place a tomato flower and a grape in the centre to resemble a blossom, if liked. Serve immediately.

Serves 3–4

MEAT

CARBONNADE OF BEEF

1 × 1.5 kg (3 lb) piece
  chuck steak
seasoned flour for coating
1 tablespoon vegetable oil
25 g (1 oz) butter
500 g (1 lb) onions, sliced
4 cloves garlic, crushed
300 ml ($^1/_2$ pint) beef
  stock, preferably
  homemade
600 ml (1 pint) brown ale
  or dark beer
1–2 tablespoons brown
  sugar
salt and pepper
1 bouquet garni
2 tablespoons wine
  vinegar
1 tablespoon freshly
  chopped parsley

Cut the beef into 10 × 5 cm (4 × 2 inch) strips and toss in the seasoned flour. Shake off any excess.

Heat the oil and butter in a large wok, add the meat in batches and stir fry until browned on all sides; drain well. Add the onions to the wok and cook for 10 minutes until golden brown, stirring occasionally. Pour off any excess fat. Return the meat to the wok, add the garlic, stock, beer and sugar. Gradually bring to the boil, season well and add the bouquet garni. Add the vinegar, cover and simmer gently for 1$^1/_2$–2 hours, stirring occasionally.

Remove the bouquet garni, transfer to a warmed serving dish and sprinkle with the parsley to serve.
Serves 4

BOEUF BOURGUIGNON

1.5 kg (3 lb) shin of beef
seasoned flour for coating
1 tablespoon vegetable oil
25 g (1 oz) butter
1 bottle red Burgundy,
  Beaujolais or Côtes-du-
  Rhone
salt and pepper
1 bouquet garni
5 cloves garlic, crushed
250 g (8 oz) button onions
350 g (12 oz) button
  mushrooms
125 g (4 oz) lean bacon,
  derinded and diced
watercress sprigs, to
  garnish

Cut the beef into 5 cm (2 inch) cubes, toss in the seasoned flour and shake off any excess.

Heat the oil and butter in a large wok, add the meat in batches and fry until browned on all sides. Pour off any excess fat from the wok.

Return the meat to the wok, add the wine, salt and pepper, bouquet garni and garlic. Slowly bring to the boil, cover and simmer gently for 1$^1/_2$ hours, until the meat is tender, stirring occasionally.

Remove the lid, stir in the onions, mushrooms and bacon, and cook for a further 15 minutes, stirring occasionally.

Remove the bouquet garni, check the seasoning and transfer to a warmed serving dish. Garnish with the watercress sprigs to serve.
Serves 4

DEEP-FRIED BEEF SLICES

4 spring onions, chopped
pinch of salt
1 tablespoon dry sherry
1 slice fresh root ginger,
　finely chopped
1 tablespoon chilli sauce
1 chilli, seeded and finely
　chopped
500 g (1 lb) rump steak,
　thinly sliced
vegetable oil for deep-
　frying
BATTER:
4 tablespoons plain flour
pinch of salt
1 egg
3–4 tablespoons water
TO GARNISH:
fresh coriander leaves
lemon slice

Put the spring onions, salt, sherry, ginger, chilli sauce and chilli in a bowl and mix well. Add the steak, toss well to coat and leave to marinate for 20–25 minutes.

Meanwhile, make the batter. Sift the flour and salt into a bowl, break in the egg and beat well, adding sufficient water to make a smooth batter.

Heat the oil in a wok to 180–190°C/350–375°F, or until a cube of bread browns in 30 seconds. Dip the steak slices into the batter and deep-fry until golden brown. Drain on kitchen paper.

Arrange the meat on a warmed serving dish and garnish with coriander and a lemon slice. Serve immediately, with soy sauce handed separately.
Serves 4–6

LAMB EN PAPILLOTE

150 ml (¼ pint) lamb
   stock
2 tablespoons red wine
8 lamb cutlets, fat
   removed
salt and pepper
1 tablespoon olive oil
1 onion, finely chopped
175 g (6 oz) fresh runner
   beans, topped, tailed
   and cut into bite-sized
   pieces
175 g (6 oz) shelled broad
   beans
125 g (4 oz) shelled fresh
   or frozen peas
4 teaspoons mint sauce
2 teaspoons redcurrant
   jelly
small sprigs of rosemary
2 cloves garlic, finely
   chopped

Boil the stock and red wine until
syrupy. Season the cutlets. Heat the
oil in a wok and stir-fry the cutlets
until golden brown. Remove the
meat from the wok and set aside. Add
the onion and stir-fry until cooked
but not brown. Pour in the stock and
bring to the boil, scraping any
sediment from the base and sides of
the wok. Keep to one side. Steam the
vegetables for 3 minutes then plunge
them in cold water.

   Cut four 35 cm (14 inch) square
pieces of foil. Arrange two lamb
cutlets and a quarter of the vegetables
on each. Divide the mint sauce,
redcurrant jelly, rosemary sprigs and
garlic among them. Pull up the sides
but leave open. Spoon on the stock
and onions and season. Seal the
parcels. Place in a steamer and cover
with a tight fitting lid. Set over a wok
of boiling water and steam for 15
minutes. Serve immediately.
Serves 4

STIR-FRIED ORANGE BEEF

2 teaspoons sesame oil
2 tablespoons dark soy
    sauce
1 tablespoon dry sherry
1 × 1 cm (¹/₂ inch) piece
    fresh root ginger, peeled
    and finely chopped
2 teaspoons cornflour
375 g (12 oz) rump steak,
    cut against the grain
    into 5 cm (2 inch) long
    thin slices
4 tablespoons vegetable oil
2 dried red chillies,
    crumbled
shredded rind of 1 orange
pinch of salt
¹/₂ teaspoon roasted
    Szechuan
    peppercorns★, finely
    ground
1 teaspoon light soft
    brown sugar
TO GARNISH:
orange slices
parsley sprigs

Mix together 1 teaspoon sesame oil, 1 tablespoon soy sauce, the sherry, ginger and cornflour. Add the meat and toss until well coated. Leave to marinate for 15 minutes; drain well.

Heat the oil in a wok and quickly brown the meat on all sides for 2 minutes; drain on kitchen paper. Pour off all but 1 tablespoon oil from the wok. Heat the wok, add the chillies and stir-fry for 30 seconds. Return the meat to the wok, add the orange rind, salt, peppercorns, sugar and remaining soy sauce. Stir-fry for 4 minutes, sprinkle with the remaining sesame oil and serve immediately, garnished with the orange slices and parsley sprigs.
Serves 4

STIR-FRIED GARLIC LAMB

2 tablespoons dry sherry
2 tablespoons light soy sauce
1 tablespoon dark soy sauce
1 teaspoon sesame oil
375 g (12 oz) lamb fillet,
    thinly sliced across the
    grain
2 tablespoons vegetable oil
6 cloves garlic, thinly
    sliced
1 × 1 cm (¹/₂ inch) piece
    fresh root ginger, peeled
    and finely chopped
1 leek, thinly sliced
    diagonally
4 spring onions, chopped
spring onion flowers★, to
    garnish

Combine the sherry, soy sauces and sesame oil, add the lamb and toss until well coated. Leave to marinate for 15 minutes, then drain, reserving the marinade.

Heat the oil in a wok, add the meat and about 2 teaspoons of the marinade and stir-fry briskly for about 2 minutes, until well browned. Add the garlic, ginger, leek and spring onions, and stir-fry for a further 3 minutes.

Transfer to a warmed serving plate, garnish with the spring onion flowers and serve immediately.
Serves 4

VEAL WITH TOMATO AND BASIL

500 g (1 lb) veal escalope,
  pounded flat and very
  thinly sliced
seasoned flour for coating
1 tablespoon vegetable oil
25 g (1 oz) butter
3 cloves garlic, crushed
6 tablespoons dry white
  wine
375 g (12 oz) tomatoes,
  skinned, seeded and
  chopped
salt and pepper
2 tablespoons chopped
  fresh basil
basil sprigs, to garnish

Toss the veal slices in seasoned flour; shake off excess.

Heat the oil and butter in a wok, add the garlic and sauté until golden; discard. Add the veal in batches and stir-fry briskly for 1 minute on each side, until lightly browned. Keep warm.

Spoon off the excess fat from the wok. Add the wine to the pan, stir well to scrape up the residue and cook for 2 minutes. Add the tomatoes, increase the heat and cook rapidly for 10–15 minutes, until thickened. Season, stir in the basil and cook for a further 5 minutes.

Arrange the veal on a serving dish. Spoon over the sauce, garnish with basil sprigs and serve at once.
Serves 4

VEAL SCALOPPINE MARSALA

500 g (1 lb) veal escalope,
  pounded flat and very
  thinly sliced
seasoned flour for coating
25 g (1 oz) butter
2 tablespoons oil
2 shallots, very finely
  chopped
8 tablespoons dry Marsala
6 tablespoons double
  cream
croûtes (see below), to
  garnish

Toss the veal slices in seasoned flour; shake off the excess.

Heat the butter and oil in a wok, add the veal in batches and stir-fry briskly for 1 minute on each side, until lightly browned. Keep warm.

Lower the heat, add the shallots to the wok and cook for 5 minutes, without browning. Spoon off excess fat. Add the Marsala, increase the heat and boil rapidly for 5 minutes, stirring occasionally, scraping up the residue. Add the cream and boil, stirring until thickened.

Arrange the scaloppine on a warmed serving plate. Spoon the sauce over the veal, garnish with the croûtes and serve immediately.
Serves 4
Note: to make croûtes: cut slices of bread into various shapes (e.g. hearts, rounds, crescents or triangles) using small cutters, and fry in butter until crisp and golden.

VEAL MOOLI

250 ml (8 fl oz) milk
4 tablespoons sunflower oil
2–4 large cloves garlic,
  chopped finely
1 large onion, chopped
  finely
750 g (1½ lb) veal
  escalope, diced
milk of 1 coconut and flesh
  of ½ a coconut or 2
  tablespoons desiccated
  coconut and 125 ml
  (4 fl oz) milk or water
1–6 fresh green chillies,
  sliced
20 strands saffron ★
  (optional)
2 tablespoons lemon juice
salt
coarsely grated coconut to
  garnish

SPICES:
¼ teaspoon asafoetida ★
  (optional)
½ teaspoon ground ginger
½ teaspoon mango
  powder ★ (optional)
½ teaspoon turmeric ★
1 teaspoon sesame seeds
1 teaspoon black mustard
  seeds ★
1 teaspoon white cumin
  seeds ★

Combine the spices with the milk to make a thin paste. Let it stand for about 30 minutes. Heat the oil in a wok and stir-fry the garlic for 1 minute. Add the onion and stir-fry for 3–4 minutes more. Blend in the spice paste. When it has reached simmering point, add the veal. Continue to simmer, stirring occasionally, for 10 minutes. Add the coconut mixture and 1–6 chillies, depending on how hot a flavour you like. The consistency of the sauce should be fairly thin. Continue to simmer for 10 minutes or until the meat is tender. Add the saffron, if using, and lemon juice and season to taste. Serve immediately, garnished with grated coconut.

Serves 4

Note: freezing is recommended. When cold store and freeze in an earthenware dish, foil or plastic container. This will keep for up to 3 months. Reheat in a covered dish in a preheated moderate oven (180°C, 350°F, Gas Mark 4) for 45 minutes or cover and microwave on Defrost for 20–25 minutes, stirring once, then reheat on High Power for 8–10 minutes, stirring twice.

FRIED PORK WITH BABY CORN

1 tablespoon dry sherry
1 tablespoon soy sauce
1¹/₂ teaspoons cornflour
500 g (1 lb) pork fillet,
  sliced as thinly as
  possible
1 tablespoon vegetable oil
50 g (2 oz) mangetout,
  trimmed
1 teaspoon salt
1 × 425 g (15 oz) can
  baby corn, drained
1 × 475 g (15 oz) can
  straw mushrooms,
  drained
2 teaspoons sugar
2 teaspoons water

Mix the sherry and soy sauce with 1 teaspoon of the cornflour. Add the pork and toss to coat thoroughly. Heat the oil in a wok. Add the pork and stir-fry until lightly browned. Add the mangetout and salt and stir-fry for 30 seconds. Add the baby corn and straw mushrooms and stir-fry for 1 minute. Sprinkle in the sugar. Mix the remaining cornflour with 2 teaspoons water and stir into the pan. Cook, stirring continuously, until thickened.

Transfer from the wok to a serving dish and serve hot.

Serves 4

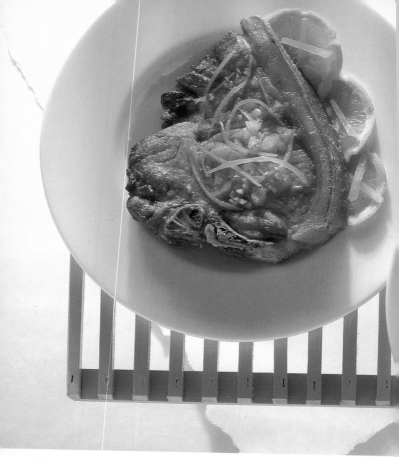

GINGER PORK WITH ORANGE

4 pork chops, about 250 g
   (8 oz) each
salt and pepper
1 tablespoon vegetable oil
1–2 cloves garlic, crushed
juice of 3 large oranges
thinly pared rind of ¹/₂
   orange, cut into
   julienne strips
2 pieces preserved stem
   ginger, chopped
1–2 tablespoons ginger
   syrup
TO GARNISH:
orange slices
slices of preserved stem
   ginger

Season the chops. Heat the oil in a
flat-bottomed wok and fry 2 chops at
a time for 4–5 minutes on each side,
until golden brown and thoroughly
cooked. Drain on kitchen paper and
keep hot on a warmed serving dish.

Pour off any excess fat from the
wok. Add the garlic, orange juice and
rind, then stir in the ginger and
syrup. Gradually bring to the boil,
stirring, then simmer for 2 minutes.

Spoon the sauce over the chops,
garnish with orange slices and ginger
and serve immediately.
Serves 4

LIVER IN ORANGE SAUCE

4 thin slices calves' liver,
    about 125 g (4 oz) each
2 tablespoons seasoned
    flour for coating
25 g (1 oz) butter
2 tablespoons olive oil
4 shallots, finely chopped
150 ml (¹/₄ pint) orange
    juice
1 teaspoon finely grated
    orange rind
salt and pepper
2 tablespoons chopped
    fresh parsley
TO GARNISH:
orange slices
parsley sprigs

Toss the liver in the seasoned flour,
shaking off any excess. Heat the
butter and oil in a flat-bottomed wok
and fry 2 pieces of liver at a time for 2
minutes on each side, until browned
on the outside and pale pink inside.
Transfer to a warmed serving dish
and keep warm.

Add the shallots to the wok and
cook for 2 minutes, without
browning. Lower the heat, add the
orange juice and rind and boil for 2
minutes, stirring. Season and stir in
the parsley. Spoon the sauce over the
liver, garnish with orange slices and
parsley and serve immediately.
Serves 4

STIR-FRIED PORK AND MANGETOUT

375 g (12 oz) lean pork,
  thinly sliced
2 tablespoons soy sauce
2 tablespoons dry sherry
4 dried Chinese
  mushrooms, soaked in
  warm water for 30
  minutes
1 tablespoon vegetable oil
250 g (8 oz) mangetout

Put the pork in a bowl with the soy sauce and sherry. Mix well to coat, then leave to marinate for 15 minutes.

Drain the mushrooms and squeeze dry. Discard the hard stalks, then slice the mushroom caps.

Heat the oil in a wok. Add the meat and marinade and stir-fry for 2 minutes. Add the mushrooms and cook for 1 minute. Add the mangetout and stir-fry for 2 minutes.

Spoon the mixture on to a warmed serving dish and serve immediately.
Serves 4–6

SWEET AND SOUR SPARE RIBS

1 kg (2 lb) lean spare ribs
salt
2 tablespoons vegetable oil
1 × 2.5 cm (1 inch) piece
  fresh root ginger, peeled
  and finely chopped
1 clove garlic, crushed
SAUCE:
4 tablespoons clear honey
4 tablespoons malt vinegar
2 tablespoons soy sauce
1 × 150 g (5 oz) can
  tomato juice
1 teaspoon mixed dried
  herbs
2 teaspoons chilli powder
dash of Worcestershire
  sauce
2 cloves garlic, crushed
TO GARNISH:
spring onion flowers★
tomato flower★

Mix all the sauce ingredients together, cover and set aside.

Cut the spare ribs into 5 cm (2 inch) pieces and sprinkle with salt. Heat the oil in a wok, add the ginger and garlic and fry for 1 minute. Add the spare ribs and fry quickly until browned. Lower the heat and cook for 10 minutes.

Spoon the sauce over the spare ribs and turn to coat them evenly. Cover the wok with foil or a lid and simmer gently for 25–30 minutes, until the meat is tender, stirring occasionally.

Arrange the spare ribs on a warmed serving dish and garnish with the spring onions and tomato flower. Serve immediately.
Serves 4–6

GIEMA CURRY

1 tablespoon olive oil
1 onion, chopped
15 g (¹/₂ oz) fresh root
   ginger, peeled and grated
2 cloves garlic, crushed
¹/₂ green pepper, seeded
   and chopped
¹/₂ red pepper, seeded and
   chopped
1 chilli, seeded and finely
   chopped
500 g (1 lb) lean lamb or
   beef, minced
salt and pepper
1 × 425 g (14 oz) can
   tomatoes
50 g (2 oz) creamed coconut
1 cinnamon stick
3 cardamom pods ★
1 clove
1 allspice berry
2 teaspoons paprika
pinch of ground fennel
pinch of cumin seeds ★
pinch of ground coriander ★
1 large potato, cubed
225 g (8 oz) shelled fresh
   or frozen peas
fresh coriander ★ leaves, to
   garnish

Heat the oil in a wok. Stir-fry the onion, ginger, garlic, peppers, chilli and meat to brown slightly. Season and remove from the heat.

Heat the tomatoes with the coconut until boiling. Stir in the spices, then pour over the meat. Add the potato and peas and mix thoroughly.

Transfer to a suitable dish. Cover with a piece of foil and tie down with string. Place on a rack or trivet in a wok half-filled with boiling water, cover with a lid and steam for 1¹/₂–1³/₄ hours. Check the liquid level frequently and add more boiling water, if necessary.

Serve from the bowl or on a bed of rice, garnished with coriander leaves.

Serves 4

Note: this traditional dish from Malaysia is best made at least a day in advance to allow the flavours to permeate the meat.

DOLMADES

12 vine, cabbage or
   spinach leaves
1 tablespoon olive oil
1 onion, finely chopped
4 tablespoons long-grain
   rice
salt and pepper
pinch of allspice
pinch of crushed rosemary
4 tablespoons lemon juice
125 g (4 oz) mushrooms,
   wiped and sliced
300 ml (½ pint) chicken
   stock
125 g (4 oz) lean minced
   lamb
2 tablespoons chopped
   parsley
25 g (1 oz) pine nuts
   (kernels)
1 teaspoon chopped fresh
   mint
lemon wedges, to garnish

Steam the leaves in a bamboo steamer
for 30 seconds over a wok half-filled
with boiling water. Lay out flat and
dry. Heat the oil in the clean wok and
stir-fry the onion and rice until lightly
coloured. Season.

Stir in the allspice, rosemary, lemon
juice, mushrooms and just enough
stock to bring the liquid 2.5 cm (1
inch) above the top of the rice. Cover
with a tight-fitting lid and cook gently
for 12 minutes. Let cool. Stir in the
lamb, parsley, nuts and mint.

Spoon about 2 teaspoons of the
mixture on to each leaf and wrap up
tightly. Pack the dolmades in layers
in the steamer and cover. Place the
remaining stock in the clean wok and
bring to the boil. Set the steamer over
the hot liquid and cook for 1 hour,
checking the liquid level frequently.

Arrange the dolmades on a dish
and garnish with lemon wedges.
Serves 4

STIR-FRIED LIVER WITH SPINACH

375 g (12 oz) pig's liver,
  cut into thin triangular
  slices
2 tablespoons cornflour
4 tablespoons vegetable oil
500 g (1 lb) fresh spinach
  leaves, rinsed and
  drained thoroughly
1 teaspoon salt
2 slices fresh root ginger,
  peeled
1 tablespoon soy sauce
1 tablespoon medium or
  dry sherry
shredded spring onion, to
  garnish

Blanch the liver for a few seconds in boiling water, then drain and coat the slices with the cornflour.

Heat 2 tablespoons of the oil in a wok. Add the spinach and salt and stir-fry for 2 minutes. Remove from the pan, then arrange around the edge of a warmed serving dish and keep hot.

Heat the remaining oil in the pan until it reaches smoking point. Add the ginger, liver, soy sauce and sherry. Avoid overcooking the liver or it will be tough. Stir-fry for 2–3 minutes, then pour into the centre of the dish.

Serve immediately, garnished with shredded spring onion.
Serves 4

AUBERGINE AND PORK IN HOT SAUCE

175 g (6 oz) boned lean
   pork, shredded
2 spring onions, finely
   chopped
1 slice fresh root ginger,
   peeled and finely
   chopped
1 clove garlic, peeled and
   finely chopped
1 tablespoon soy sauce
1 teaspoon medium or dry
   sherry
1¹/₂ teaspoons cornflour
vegetable oil for deep-
   frying
250 g (8 oz) aubergine,
   cut into diamond-
   shaped chunks
1 tablespoon chilli sauce
3–4 tablespoons chicken
   stock or water
chopped spring onion, to
   garnish

Put the pork in a bowl with the
spring onions, ginger, garlic, soy
sauce, sherry and cornflour. Mix
well, then leave to marinate for about
20 minutes.

Heat the oil in a wok to
180–190°C/350–375°F, or until a
cube of bread browns in 30 seconds.
Lower the heat, add the aubergine
and deep-fry for about 1¹/₂ minutes.
Remove from the pan with a slotted
spoon and drain on kitchen paper.

Pour off all but 1 tablespoon of the
oil from the wok, then add the pork
and stir-fry for about 1 minute. Add
the aubergine and chilli sauce and
cook for about 1¹/₂ minutes, then
moisten with the stock or water.
Simmer until the liquid has almost
completely evaporated. Serve hot,
garnished with chopped spring
onions.
Serves 3–4

51

POULTRY AND GAME
CHICKEN IN GRAND MARNIER

4 boneless chicken breasts,
  skinned
seasoned flour for coating
50 g (2 oz) butter
4 shallots, finely chopped
6 tablespoons Grand
  Marnier
3 tablespoons chicken
  stock, preferably
  homemade
1 bouquet garni
salt and pepper
250 ml (8 fl oz) double
  cream
25 g (1 oz) flaked
  almonds, toasted
small bunches of mixed
  herbs, to garnish

Toss the chicken in the flour. Melt the butter in a wok, add the chicken and brown on all sides; drain.

Add the shallots to the wok and cook for 2 minutes. Return the chicken to the wok, pour over half the Grand Marnier and the stock. Add the bouquet garni and season. Bring to the boil, then cover and simmer for 20–25 minutes, until the chicken is tender. Transfer to a serving dish and keep warm. Remove the bouquet garni.

Add the remaining Grand Marnier to the wok, increase the heat and boil rapidly until the liquid has reduced by half. Add the cream and boil for 1 minute, then spoon over the chicken. Sprinkle with the toasted almonds and garnish with the herbs.
Serves 4

SICILIAN CHICKEN

4 boneless chicken breasts,
  skinned
seasoned flour for coating
50 g (2 oz) butter
250 g (8 oz) button onions
6 tablespoons Marsala
250 g (8 oz) tomatoes,
  skinned, seeded and
  chopped
pinch of dried mixed herbs
2 tablespoons chicken
  stock, preferably
  homemade
salt and pepper
1 tablespoon chopped
  parsley
croûtes (see page 40), to
  garnish

Toss the chicken in seasoned flour. Melt the butter in a wok, add the onions and cook for 2–3 minutes, until lightly browned. Remove from the wok and set aside. Increase the heat, add the chicken and brown on all sides. Pour off any excess fat. Return the onions to the wok, add the Marsala, tomatoes, herbs and stock and season well. Bring slowly to the boil, cover tightly with a lid or foil and simmer for 20 minutes, until the chicken is tender. Lift the chicken on to a warmed serving dish.

Increase the heat and boil the sauce in the wok rapidly for about 5 minutes, stirring occasionally, until thickened. Stir in the parsley. Spoon over the chicken and garnish with croûtes.
Serves 4

LEMON-SCENTED POUSSIN

4 × 375 g (12 oz)
  poussin, washed and
  dried
grated rind of 1 lemon
4 tablespoons lemon juice
150 ml (¹/₄ pint) dry white
  wine
sprigs of thyme, marjoram
  and oregano for the
  marinade
salt and pepper
2 tablespoons olive oil
¹/₂ red cabbage, cut into
  julienne strips
4 tablespoons chopped
  fresh thyme, marjoram
  and oregano
150 ml (¹/₄ pint) double
  cream
600 ml (1 pint) chicken
  stock
sprig of lemon grass
sprigs or chopped fresh
  mixed herbs, to garnish

Place the poussin in a dish with the lemon rind and juice, white wine and herbs. Season well and leave to marinate for up to 2 hours. Remove from the marinade and dry well. Heat the oil in a wok and stir-fry the poussin over high heat until golden brown on all sides.

Line a bamboo steamer with a sheet of non-stick parchment and arrange the red and white cabbage over the paper. Top with the four poussin. Season well and spoon over the chopped fresh herbs. Pour the remaining marinade into the clean wok with the double cream, chicken stock and lemon grass. Cover the steamer with a tight-fitting lid and steam over the stock for 40–45 minutes. Check the liquid level frequently.

Arrange each poussin on a bed of mixed cabbage on individual plates and keep warm. Remove the lemon grass and reduce the stock until rich and creamy. Pour over the poussin and garnish with sprigs of herbs.
Serves 4

CHICKEN IN LETTUCE

600 ml (1 pint) chicken
  stock
300 ml (1/2 pint) dry cider
8 large cos lettuce leaves,
  washed
4 boneless chicken breasts,
  skinned
50 g (2 oz) butter,
  softened
2 cloves garlic, crushed
salt and pepper
2 large carrots, cut into
  matchsticks
2 celery sticks, cut into
  matchsticks
50 g (2 oz) smoked ham,
  cut into strips
4 tablespoons lemon juice
125 g (4 oz) unsalted
  butter, cut into walnut-
  sized pieces
fennel, to garnish

Bring the chicken stock and cider to the boil in a wok. Steam the lettuce leaves over the stock and cider for 20 seconds or until just limp. Dry.

Spread the chicken breasts with the softened butter and garlic and season. Lay down the lettuce leaves in pairs, overlapping slightly. Lay each chicken breast at the stalk end of the leaves. Divide three-quarters of the vegetables and all of the ham between the four breasts.

Blanch the remaining vegetables, drain, then put to one side for the garnish. Squeeze the lemon juice over the chicken, fold the leaves over the mixture and place each parcel in the steamer. Cover, and steam over the cider and stock for 20 minutes.

When cooked, remove the chicken parcels and keep warm. Reduce the stock until syrupy. Lower the heat and whisk in the butter pieces, until you have a smooth, creamy sauce. Check the seasoning.

Flood four plates with cider sauce, then lay the chicken parcels on top. Garnish with the remaining vegetables and fennel.
Serves 4

SPICY CHICKEN AND PEANUTS

125 g (4 oz) unsalted peanuts
2 tablespoons vegetable oil
1 dried red chilli
375 g (12 oz) boneless
   chicken breast, skinned
   and cut into 2.5 cm
   (1 inch) cubes
2 tablespoons dry sherry
1 tablespoon dark soy sauce
pinch of sugar
1 clove garlic, crushed
2 spring onions, chopped
1 × 2.5 cm (1 inch) piece
   fresh root ginger, peeled
   and finely chopped
1 teaspoon wine vinegar
2 teaspoons sesame oil
red chilli flowers, ★ to
   garnish

Immerse the peanuts in a bowl of boiling water for about 2 minutes. Drain well, remove the skins and place on kitchen paper to dry.

Heat the oil in a wok. Crumble in the chilli, add the chicken and peanuts and stir-fry for 1 minute; remove from the wok. Place the sherry, soy sauce, sugar, garlic, spring onions, ginger and vinegar in the wok. Bring to the boil, then simmer for 30 seconds. Return the chicken, chilli and peanuts to the wok and cook for 2 minutes. Sprinkle over the sesame oil.

Pile into a warmed serving dish, garnish with red chilli flowers and serve immediately.
Serves 4

CASHEW CHICKEN

1 egg white
4 tablespoons dry sherry
2 teaspoons cornflour
375 g (12 oz) boneless
    chicken breast, skinned
    and cut into 1 cm
    (¹/₂ inch) cubes
3 tablespoons vegetable oil
4 spring onions, chopped
2 cloves garlic, thinly
    sliced
1 × 2.5 cm (1 inch) piece
    fresh root ginger, peeled
    and finely chopped
1 tablespoon light soy
    sauce
125 g (4 oz) unsalted
    cashew nuts

Combine the egg white, half the
sherry and the cornflour, add the
chicken and toss well until evenly
coated.

Heat the oil in a wok, add the
spring onions, garlic and ginger and
stir-fry for 30 seconds. Add the
chicken and cook for 2 minutes. Pour
in the remaining sherry and the soy
sauce and stir well. Add the cashew
nuts and cook for a further 30
seconds. Serve immediately.
Serves 4

CHICKEN JALFREZI

6 tablespoons clarified
   butter or ghee★
2–6 cloves garlic, chopped
   finely
1 × 5 cm (2 inch) piece
   fresh root ginger, peeled
   and sliced finely
1 large onion, sliced thinly
750 g (1¹/₂ lb) boneless
   chicken breast, skinned
   and diced
1 tablespoon mild curry
   paste★
¹/₂ red pepper, seeded and
   chopped
¹/₂ green pepper, seeded
   and chopped
2 tomatoes, skinned and
   chopped
1 tablespoon chopped fresh
   coriander leaves★
1–2 tablespoons water
SPICES:
1 teaspoon white cumin
   seeds★
1 teaspoon black mustard
   seeds★

Heat the butter or ghee in a wok and
stir-fry the spices for 1 minute. Add
the garlic and stir-fry for 1 minute
more. Add the ginger and stir-fry for
2 minutes. Add the sliced onion and
stir-fry until golden – about 5
minutes.

Combine the chicken pieces with
the ingredients in the wok, stirring
and turning for 5 more minutes. Add
all the remaining ingredients and stir-
fry for about 10 more minutes. Serve
immediately.

Serves 4
Note: freezing is recommended.
When cold store and freeze in an
earthenware dish, foil or plastic
container. This will keep for up to 3
months. Reheat in a covered dish in a
preheated moderate oven (180°C,
350°F, Gas Mark 4) for 45 minutes or
cover and microwave on Defrost for
20–25 minutes, stirring once, then
reheat on High Power for 8–10
minutes, stirring twice.

COCONUT CHICKEN

6 tablespoons sunflower
  oil
750 g (1¹/₂ lb) boneless
  chicken breast, skinned
  and diced
2–6 cloves garlic, chopped
  finely
300 ml (¹/₂ pint) milk
50 ml (2 fl oz) natural
  yogurt
2 tablespoons desiccated
  coconut
1 tablespoon chopped fresh
  coriander★ (if
  available)
salt

SPICES:
1 teaspoon black mustard
  seeds★
1 teaspoon sesame seeds
1 teaspoon poppy seeds
¹/₂ teaspoon black cumin
  seeds★

TO GARNISH:
20 unsalted cashew nuts,
  fried until golden
coriander sprigs

Heat the oil in a wok and stir-fry the
spices for 1 minute. Add the chicken
and stir-fry for about 5 minutes,
turning frequently, until it is white all
over. Add the garlic, milk, yogurt
and coconut. Simmer for 5 minutes,
stirring from time to time. Add the
coriander and simmer for 5–10
minutes, until the chicken is tender.
Season to taste. Transfer to a heated
dish. Garnish with fried cashews and
sprigs of coriander.
Serves 4
Note: freezing is recommended.
When cold, freeze in a plastic
container. This will keep for up to 3
months. Reheat in a covered dish in a
preheated moderate oven (180°C,
350°F, Gas Mark 4) for 45 minutes or
cover and microwave on Defrost for
20–25 minutes, stirring once, then
reheat on High Power for 8–10
minutes, stirring twice.

STEWED CHICKEN WITH CHESTNUTS

6 tablespoons soy sauce
1 tablespoon dry sherry
1 × 1 kg (2 lb) chicken,
    boned and cut into 4 cm
    (1¹/₂ inch) pieces
2 tablespoons vegetable oil
2 slices fresh root ginger,
    peeled and chopped
4 spring onions, chopped
500 g (1 lb) chestnuts,
    peeled and skinned
450 ml (³/₄ pint) water
1 tablespoon sugar

Mix together the soy sauce and sherry in a dish and add the chicken. Leave to marinate for 15 minutes.

Heat the oil in a wok. Add the chicken mixture, ginger and half of the spring onions; stir-fry until the chicken is golden. Add the chestnuts, water and sugar. Bring to the boil, cover and simmer for 40 minutes or until tender. Serve hot, garnished with the remaining spring onions.
Serves 4

FRIED EIGHT-PIECE CHICKEN

2–3 spring onions, finely
  chopped
2–3 slices fresh root
  ginger, peeled and
  finely chopped
2 tablespoons dry sherry
1 tablespoon sugar
3 tablespoons soy sauce
1 × 1.25 kg (2½ lb)
  spring chicken, jointed
  and breasts cut in half
3 tablespoons cornflour
4 tablespoons vegetable oil
1 teaspoon sesame oil
chopped parsley, to
  garnish

Mix the spring onions and ginger
with 1 tablespoon sherry, 1 teaspoon
sugar and 1 tablespoon soy sauce.
Add the chicken pieces and leave to
marinate for 3 minutes.

Coat each piece of chicken with
cornflour. Heat the vegetable oil in a
wok. Add the chicken pieces and stir-
fry until golden and cooked through.
Pour off the excess oil and add the
remaining sherry, sugar and soy
sauce to the pan. Bring to the boil,
stirring. Add the sesame seed oil just
before serving, and garnish with
parsley.
Serves 4

61

CHICKEN FRITTERS

5 egg whites
125 ml (4 fl oz) chicken
   stock
1 teaspoon salt
1 teaspoon rice wine or
   sherry
2 teaspoons cornflour
125 g (4 oz) boneless
   chicken breast, skinned
   and finely chopped
vegetable oil for deep-
   frying
TO GARNISH:
1–2 tablespoons cooked
   peas
25 g (1 oz) cooked ham,
   shredded

Put the egg whites in a bowl. Stir in 3 tablespoons of the chicken stock, the salt, wine and half the cornflour. Add the chicken and mix well.

Heat the oil in a wok to 180–190°C/350–375°F, or until a cube of bread browns in 30 seconds. Gently pour in about one-third of the egg and chicken mixture. Deep-fry for 10 seconds until the mixture begins to rise to the surface, then carefully turn it over. Deep-fry until golden. Remove from the wok, drain and place on a warmed serving dish. Keep hot while cooking the remainder in the same way.

Heat the remaining stock in a small pan. Mix the remaining cornflour to a paste with a little cold water, add to the stock and simmer, stirring, until thickened. Pour over the chicken. Garnish with peas and ham. Serve hot.
Serves 4

FOIL-WRAPPED CHICKEN

500 g (1 lb) boneless
  chicken breast, skinned
  and cut into 12 pieces
3 spring onions, white
  part only, cut into 4
  pieces each
1/4 teaspoon salt
1 tablespoon soy sauce
1 teaspoon sugar
1 teaspoon rice wine or
  sherry
1 teaspoon sesame oil
4 tablespoons vegetable oil
TO GARNISH:
shredded spring onion
finely chopped red pepper

Combine the chicken and spring onions with the salt, soy sauce, sugar, wine and sesame oil in a bowl. Leave to marinate for about 20 minutes.

Cut 12 squares of foil large enough to wrap around the chicken pieces four times. Brush the pieces of foil with oil, then place a piece of chicken on each. Top with a piece of spring onion, then wrap the foil around the chicken to make a parcel, completely enclosing it.

Heat the oil in a wok and fry the chicken parcels over moderate heat for about 2 minutes on each side. Remove and leave to drain on a rack for a few minutes; turn off the heat.

Reheat the oil. When very hot, return the chicken parcels to the wok and fry for 1 minute only. Serve hot in the foil, garnished with shredded spring onion and red pepper.
Serves 4

DICED TURKEY WITH CELERY

4 dried Chinese
    mushrooms, soaked in
    warm water for 30
    minutes
375 g (12 oz) boneless
    turkey breast, skinned
    and diced
salt
1 egg white
1 tablespoon cornflour
4 tablespoons vegetable oil
2 cloves garlic, sliced
2 slices fresh root ginger,
    peeled and finely
    chopped
2 leeks, diagonally sliced
1 small head celery,
    diagonally sliced
1 red pepper, cored, seeded
    and sliced
3 tablespoons light soy sauce
2 tablespoons dry sherry
celery leaves, to garnish

Drain the mushrooms and squeeze dry. Discard the hard stalks, then slice the mushroom caps.

Season the diced turkey with salt, dip in the egg white, then coat with cornflour. Heat the oil in a wok. Add the turkey and stir-fry for 1 minute, until golden brown. Remove with a slotted spoon and drain on kitchen paper.

Increase the heat. Add the garlic, ginger, leeks and celery and stir-fry for 1 minute. Return the turkey to the wok, add the red pepper and stir-fry for 30 seconds. Stir in the soy sauce and sherry and cook for a further 30 seconds. Spoon into a warmed serving dish, garnish with celery leaves and serve immediately.

Serves 4

TURKEY PARCELS

1 tablespoon soy sauce
1 tablespoon dry sherry
1 tablespoon sesame oil
500 g (1 lb) boned turkey
    breast, skinned and cut
    into 16 equal pieces
4 spring onions, each cut
    into 4 pieces
2 × 2.5 cm (1 inch) pieces
    fresh root ginger, peeled
    and shredded
$^{1}/_{2}$ red pepper, cored,
    seeded and shredded
1 celery stick, shredded
4 tablespoons vegetable oil

Mix the soy sauce, sherry and sesame oil together, add the turkey and toss well to coat. Leave to marinate for 15–20 minutes.

Cut out 16 pieces of foil large enough to enclose the pieces of turkey generously. Brush the foil with oil, place a piece of turkey in the centre of each one and top with a piece of spring onion, ginger, pepper and celery. Fold the foil over to enclose the turkey and seal the edges well.

Heat the oil in a wok, add the foil parcels and fry for about 2 minutes each side. Remove from the wok and leave to drain.

Reheat the oil to very hot and return the turkey parcels to the wok for 1 minute. Drain well and serve immediately in the silver parcels.

Serves 4

STEAMED WILD DUCK LIVERS

500 g (1 lb) duck livers,
  washed and trimmed
50 ml (2 fl oz) milk
300 ml (¹/₂ pint) duck or
  chicken stock
3 spring onions, trimmed
  and sliced
1 carrot, finely diced
salt and pepper
1 tablespoon honey
2 teaspoons red wine
  vinegar
small head of radiccio,
  washed and divided into
  separate leaves
bunch watercress
TO GARNISH:
50 g (2 oz) smoked ham,
  cut into strips
  (optional)
finely chopped spring
  onion tips (optional)

Wild duck livers are indescribably delicious but not always easy to get hold of. Use normal duck livers if necessary; you won't be too disappointed!

Soak the livers in the milk for 30 minutes. Discard the milk, rinse the livers and pat dry. Bring the stock to the boil in the wok. Lay a sheet of wet greaseproof paper in a bamboo steamer. Place the livers, spring onion and carrot on top. Season well.

Steam over the stock for 5 minutes. Remove the liver and vegetables, set aside and keep warm. Add the honey and vinegar to the stock. Boil to reduce until syrupy.

Arrange the radiccio and watercress on four plates, then spoon on the liver and vegetables. Pour on the sauce. Sprinkle with strips of ham and spring onion tips, if liked. Serve at once.

Serves 4

DUCK WITH CRACKED PEPPER AND APPLES

4 Granny Smith apples,
  peeled and cored but
  kept whole
4 tablespoons lemon juice
1 tablespoon whole black
  peppercorns, crushed
600 ml (1 pint) red wine
2 tablespoons Calvados
  brandy
2 shallots, finely chopped
4 duck breasts, wiped
salt
1 tablespoon olive oil
150 ml (1/4 pint) chicken
  or game stock
50 ml (2 fl oz) double
  cream
sprigs of herbs, to garnish,
  e.g. chervil, flat-leaf
  parsley, fennel

Brush the apples with lemon juice. Put the apples, peppercorns, wine, Calvados, shallots and duck breasts in a shallow dish. Marinate for 2 hours, turning the large pieces frequently.

Remove the duck breasts and apples from the marinade and reserve the liquid. Dry the duck on kitchen paper and sprinkle with a little salt. Heat the oil in a wok and stir-fry the duck breasts until golden brown on all sides. Place in a steamer with the apples. Place the remaining marinade, stock and cream in the cleaned wok and bring to the boil. Steam the duck over the stock mixture for 10–12 minutes. Slice the apples. Arrange the duck and apples on a warmed serving dish and keep hot. Reduce the peppered stock by boiling until syrupy. Taste and adjust seasoning. Spoon the sauce over the duck and garnish with sprigs of herbs.
Serves 4

DUCK WITH ALMONDS

500 g (1 lb) lean duck
   meat, cut into chunks
2 slices fresh root ginger,
   peeled and shredded
1 clove garlic, crushed
3 tablespoons vegetable oil
3–4 dried Chinese
   mushrooms, soaked in
   warm water for 30
   minutes
4 spring onions, sliced
125 g (4 oz) canned
   bamboo shoots, drained
   and sliced
3 tablespoons soy sauce
2 tablespoons sherry
2 teaspoons cornflour
25 g (1 oz) flaked
   almonds, toasted

Place the duck pieces in a bowl with the ginger and garlic. Pour over 1 tablespoon of the oil and leave to marinate for 30 minutes.

Drain the mushrooms and squeeze them dry. Discard the hard stalks, then slice the mushroom caps.

Heat the remaining oil in a wok, add the spring onions and stir-fry for 30 seconds. Add the duck and cook for 2 minutes. Add the mushrooms, bamboo shoots, soy sauce and sherry and cook for 2 minutes. Blend the cornflour with 1 tablespoon water and stir into the pan. Cook for 1 minute, stirring, until thickened.

Stir in the toasted almonds and serve immediately.

Serves 4–6

CRISPY DUCKLING

1 × 2 kg (4 lb) duckling
vegetable oil for deep-
    frying
MASTER SAUCE:
1.2 litres (2 pints) stock
600 ml (1 pint) Chinese
    wine or dry sherry
7 tablespoons soy sauce
4 tablespoons hoisin
    sauce★
4 onions, sliced
6 slices fresh root ginger,
    peeled
1¹/₂ tablespoons sugar
6 garlic cloves, crushed
1 chicken stock cube
1 teaspoon five-spice
    powder★
1 kg (2 lb) pork bones
500 g (1 lb) shin of beef,
    cubed
TO SERVE:
10–12 Mandarin
    pancakes★
5 tablespoons hoisin
    sauce★
2 cucumbers, peeled and
    sliced lengthwise
4–5 spring onions,
    shredded

Plunge the duckling into a wok of boiling water. Boil for 10 minutes, then drain.

Combine the sauce ingredients in a wok. Bring to the boil, cover and simmer for 30 minutes; discard the bones. Add the duckling to the sauce and coat thoroughly. Bring to the boil, cover and simer gently for 1¹/₂ hours, turning the duckling a few times during cooking. Lift the duckling out of the sauce and transfer to a wire rack to drain thoroughly while cooling.

When the duckling is thoroughly dry, heat the oil in a wok to 180–190°C/350–375°F, or until a cube of bread browns in 30 seconds. Lower the duckling into the oil and deep-fry for 8–10 minutes, spooning the oil over the exposed surface of the duckling. Drain and place on a serving dish. If liked, the duckling may be garnished with cucumber slices, strips of lemon rind and parsley sprigs. Serve hot with the accompaniments. The meat should be tender enough to be taken off the bone with chopsticks.
Serves 6

VEGETABLES

INDONESIAN VEGETABLE CURRY

4 tablespoons vegetable oil
3–4 tablespoons fresh
    lemon juice
300 g (10 oz) aubergines,
    chopped
300 g (10 oz) courgettes,
    sliced
1 head of Chinese leaves,
    bottom half only,
    chopped
1 tablespoon brown sugar
salt

SPICE PASTE:
2–6 cloves garlic
1 large onion, finely chopped
1 × 2.5 cm (1 inch) piece
    fresh root ginger, peeled
1 red pepper, cored, seeded
    and chopped
2–6 fresh red chillies,
    chopped
10 unsalted cashew nuts or
    candlenuts
1 teaspoon pepper
1 teaspoon turmeric★

Place all the ingredients for the spice paste into a blender and blend to a fairly stiff consistency, using as little water as possible. Heat the oil in a wok. Stir-fry the paste for 5 minutes, adding the lemon juice a little at a time, so that it is incorporated smoothly. Stir in enough water to make the sauce a pouring consistency. Add the aubergines, courgettes and Chinese leaves. Simmer for 5–10 minutes, until the aubergines are tender. Stir in the brown sugar and season with salt to taste. Serve at once.

Serves 4

THAI VEGETABLE CURRY

175 ml (6 fl oz) water
4 tablespoons thinly pared
    lemon rind
4 tablespoons vegetable oil
2 puréed anchovies
2 tablespoons desiccated
    coconut
1 × 175 g (6 oz) can
    water chestnuts
475 g (15 oz) baby
    sweetcorn cobs
175 g (6 oz) bamboo
    shoots, sliced
GREEN PURÉE:
1 green pepper
1–6 green chillies
1 bunch watercress
2 tablespoons chopped
    fresh coriander*
4 spinach leaves
2–4 cloves garlic
1 × 5 cm (2 inch) piece
    fresh root ginger, peeled
TO GARNISH:
lime wedges
basil sprigs

Place the water in a saucepan with the lemon rind and boil for 1 minute. Remove from the heat and set aside for the flavour to infuse.

Place the ingredients for the green purée into a liquidizer and process until smooth, using a little water if necessary. Heat the oil in a wok and stir-fry the green purée for 5–6 minutes. Strain the lemon water into the wok and add the puréed anchovies and coconut mixed with water to a runny paste. Combine well to give a smooth mixture. Add the water chestnuts, baby sweetcorn cobs and bamboo shoots. If you are using canned vegetables, use some of their liquid for stock – enough to make the curry runny but not watery. Simmer the vegetables for 5–6 minutes. To serve, garnish with lime wedges and sprigs of basil.
Serves 4

STIR-FRIED GARLIC SPINACH

1 kg (2 lb) spinach
2 tablespoons vegetable oil
4 spring onions, chopped
1 teaspoon light soy sauce
pinch of sugar
pinch of salt
2 cloves garlic, crushed
1 teaspoon toasted sesame
   seeds

Wash the spinach thoroughly and remove all the stems. Drain well.

Heat the oil in a large wok, add the spring onions and fry for 30 seconds. Add the spinach and stir-fry for about 2 minutes, until the leaves are coated in the oil and have wilted. Add the soy sauce, sugar, salt and garlic and continue stir-frying for 3 minutes. Pour off any excess liquid.

Transfer to a warmed serving dish and sprinkle with sesame seeds.
Serves 4

STIR-FRIED GINGER BROCCOLI

500 g (1 lb) broccoli,
    divided into florets,
    stems peeled and sliced
salt
2 tablespoons vegetable oil
1 clove garlic, thinly sliced
    (optional)
1 × 2.5 cm (1 inch) piece
    fresh root ginger, peeled
    and finely shredded
1/2–1 teaspoon sesame oil

Blanch the broccoli in boiling salted water for 30 seconds, drain well and cool rapidly under cold running water; drain thoroughly.

Heat the oil in a wok, add the garlic and ginger and stir-fry for 2–3 seconds. Add the blanched broccoli and cook for 2 minutes. Sprinkle over the sesame oil and stir-fry for a further 30 seconds.

Spoon into a warmed serving dish and serve immediately.
Serves 4

NEST OF BABY VEGETABLES

12 baby carrots, washed
12 baby turnips, washed
50 g (2 oz) mangetout,
   topped and tailed
100 g (4 oz) French
   beans, topped and tailed
8 button onions
8 radishes, washed
50 g (2 oz) butter
4 tablespoons white wine
4 strips lemon zest
4 teaspoons chopped fresh
   herbs, for example,
   chervil, chives, mint
salt and pepper

Fold 8 sheets of greaseproof paper in half, cut out a semi-circle of 15 cm (6 inch) radius through each so that when opened you have 8 × 30 cm (12 inch) rounds of paper.

Place the circles together in pairs so that you have 4 double-thick circles.

Divide all of the ingredients between the 4 circles, arranging the food on one half of each circle only, and season well. Fold the free half over to make a parcel rather like an apple turnover. Fold the edges of the layers of paper over twice together, twisting and pressing hard to make an air-tight seal.

Lay the parcels inside a steamer. Cover with a tight-fitting lid and steam over a wok of boiling water for 8–10 minutes.

Serve at once, letting diners open the envelopes at the table.

Serves 4

PROVENCAL VEGETABLE SALAD

1 × 50 g (2 oz) can
   anchovy fillets, drained
a little milk
$^1/_2$ yellow pepper, cored,
   seeded and cut into
   matchsticks
$^1/_2$ red pepper, cored,
   seeded and cut into
   matchsticks
$^1/_2$ green pepper, cored,
   seeded and cut into
   matchsticks
small bulb of fennel, cut
   into chunks
$^1/_2$ cauliflower, divided
   into florets
250 g (8 oz) broccoli,
   divided into florets
125 g (4 oz) cap
   mushrooms, wiped
8 cherry tomatoes
125 g (4 oz) runner
   beans, halved
6 tablespoons olive oil
3 tablespoons red wine
   vinegar
$^1/_2$ teaspoon fresh thyme
   leaves
1 tablespoon chopped fresh
   basil
1 tablespoon Dijon
   mustard
salt and pepper

Soak the anchovies in a little milk for 30 minutes. Drain and rinse in cold water. Place all the vegetables in a bamboo steamer set over a wok of boiling water and steam for 3–5 minutes.

Meanwhile make the dressing. Place the anchovies, olive oil, vinegar, thyme, basil and mustard in a liquidizer or food processor. Blend for a few seconds, then season well.

Toss the warm vegetables with the dressing and serve immediately, with crusty brown bread and butter, if liked.

Serves 4

BAKED STUFFED TOMATOES

3 dried Chinese mushrooms,
  soaked in warm water
  for 30 minutes
1 tablespoon oil
1 large onion, finely
  chopped
500 g (1 lb) minced beef or
  pork
50 g (2 oz) canned water
  chestnuts, drained and
  chopped
2 tablespoons soy sauce
2 tablespoons dry sherry
8 large tomatoes
1 tablespoon cornflour,
  blended with 2
  tablespoons water
fresh coriander leaves★ to
  garnish

Drain the mushrooms, and squeeze dry. Discard stalks and chop the caps.

Heat the oil in a wok, add the onion and stir-fry until browned. Add the meat and cook, stirring, for 5 minutes until browned. Stir in the mushrooms, water chestnuts, soy sauce and sherry. Cook for 2 minutes.

Cut the tomatoes in half, scoop out the flesh and add to the wok, discarding the seeds. Stir in the blended cornflour and cook, stirring, for 1 minute. Spoon the mixture into the tomato halves. Cook in a preheated moderate oven, 180°C, 350°F, Gas Mark 4, for 15–20 minutes, until tender. Serve hot, garnished with coriander.

Serves 4–8

STUFFED GREEN PEPPERS

1 tablespoon vegetable oil
1 clove garlic, crushed
1 × 2.5 cm (1 inch) piece
  fresh root ginger, peeled
  and finely chopped
250 g (8 oz) minced pork
1 spring onion, chopped
1 celery stick, finely
  chopped
grated rind of 1 lemon
4 green peppers, cored,
  seeded and quartered

Heat the oil in a wok, add the garlic and stir-fry until lightly browned. Lower the heat, add the ginger and pork and cook for 2 minutes. Stir in the spring onion, celery and lemon rind, and mix well and cook for 30 seconds. Cool slightly.

Divide the mixture between the pepper quarters, pressing it well into the cavity.

Arrange the pepper quarters in an oiled ovenproof dish. Cook in a preheated moderately hot oven, 200°C, 400°F, Gas Mark 6, for 20–25 minutes, until tender. Transfer to a warmed serving dish and serve immediately.

Serves 4–6

SWEET AND SOUR ONIONS

1.5 kg (3 lb) small white
  onions
50 g (2 oz) butter
2¹/₂ tablespoons white
  wine vinegar
2 teaspoons sugar
salt and pepper
1 tablespoon chopped fresh
  parsley

Plunge the onions into boiling water for 15 seconds. Drain well and leave for about 10 minutes, until they are sufficiently cool to handle. Remove just the outer skin and roots; do not peel away any of the layers, and leave the base of the root intact to keep the onion together during cooking. Cut a cross in the root end.

Melt the butter in a wok, add the onions and sufficient water just to cover the onions – about 2.5 cm (1 inch) depth. Bring to the boil, stirring occasionally, then lower the heat and simmer for 20 minutes.

Add the vinegar, sugar and salt and pepper and stir well. Simmer very gently for 1¹/₂–2 hours, stirring frequently; add a tablespoon of water from time to time if necessary. The onions should be a rich, dark golden brown all over and tender when cooked.

Transfer to a warmed serving dish, sprinkle with parsley and serve immediately.
Serves 4

MUSHROOMS WITH CREAM

50 g (2 oz) butter
2–3 shallots, very finely
  chopped
750 g (1¹/₂ lb) small button
  mushrooms
2 tablespoons dry white
  vermouth
150 ml (5 fl oz) double
  cream
salt and pepper
2 tablespoons freshly
  chopped chives

Melt the butter in a wok, add the shallots and stir-fry for about 5 minutes, until golden brown, stirring constantly. Add the mushrooms and stir well to coat them in the butter. Lower the heat and cook for a further 3–4 minutes.

Increase the heat, add the vermouth and boil rapidly for 1–2 minutes, until reduced. Pour in the cream and cook for 2 minutes, until thickened, then season. Transfer to a warmed serving dish, sprinkle with the chives and serve immediately.
Serves 4

POTATO GALETTE

250–300 g (8–10 oz)
  potatoes, peeled and
  very thinly sliced
125 g (4 oz) butter,
  melted
salt
parsley or coriander, to
  garnish

Place the potatoes in a bowl of cold water and rinse well. Pour half the butter into a flat-bottomed wok.

Drain the potatoes well and dry on kitchen paper. Arrange the slices in the pan, overlapping slightly like the scales of a fish. Spoon over some more butter. Continue layering the potato slices and butter. Cook over moderate heat for about 2 minutes, shaking the pan with a circular movement to prevent the potatoes from sticking. Press down the galette with the back of a spoon and cook for 10 minutes. Turn over and cook the other side for 10 minutes.

Drain off the butter, tilting the pan but keeping the galette in position. Slide on to a warmed serving plate and serve immediately, garnished with parsley or coriander.

Serves 4

POTATO PANCAKES

500 g (1 lb) potatoes
4 tablespoons boiling milk
4 tablespoons plain flour
3 eggs
4 egg whites
$1/2$ teaspoon dried mixed
  herbs (optional)
4 tablespoons double
  cream
salt and pepper
vegetable oil for frying
parsley sprig, to garnish

Boil the potatoes in their skins until tender. Remove the skins, then mash the potatoes until very smooth. Beat in the boiling milk and leave to cool.

Using a wooden spoon, beat in the flour, whole eggs and egg whites. Stir in the herbs, if using, and cream, and season. Beat until very smooth – it should resemble a thick batter.

Heat the oil in a flat-bottomed wok, swirling it around just to cover the base. When it begins to give off a slight haze, drop in tablespoons of the batter, and cook for 2 minutes on each side, until golden brown.

Place the pancakes in layers in a clean dry tea-towel and put into a cool oven to keep warm. Repeat with the remaining batter.

Serve very hot, garnished with parsley.

Serves 4

DEEP-FRIED GREEN BEANS

600 ml (1 pint) vegetable
   oil for deep-frying
500 g (1 lb) French beans
3 cloves garlic, crushed
1 tablespoon chopped root
   ginger
4 spring onions, chopped
4 dried red chillies
1 tablespoon whole yellow
   bean sauce
1 tablespoon dry sherry
1 tablespoon dark soy
   sauce
pinch of sugar
1 tablespoon stock

Heat the oil in a deep-fat fryer or wok until a single bean dropped into the oil sizzles. Deep-fry half the beans for about 3–4 minutes, until they are slightly wrinkled; remove and drain well. Repeat with the remaining beans.

Transfer about 1 tablespoon of the oil to a wok and heat. Add the garlic, ginger and spring onions and stir-fry for 5 seconds. Add the chillies and cook for a further 30 seconds, until they turn black. Remove the chillies, then add the remaining ingredients and stir-fry for a few seconds. Stir in the drained beans and stir-fry for 2 minutes, until they are hot and coated in the sauce.

Transfer to a warmed serving dish and serve immediately.

Serves 4

STIR-FRIED SPICED CUCUMBER

$1^1/_2$ cucumbers
2 teaspoons salt
1 tablespoon oil
$^1/_4$ teaspoon chilli bean
   sauce or chilli powder
6 cloves garlic, crushed
$1^1/_2$ tablespoons black
   beans, coarsely chopped
5 tablespoons chicken
   stock
1 teaspoon sesame oil
cucumber slices, to garnish

Peel the cucumbers, slice in half lengthways, remove the seeds, then cut into 2.5 cm (1 inch) cubes. Sprinkle with salt and leave to drain in a colander for about 30 minutes. Rinse in cold water, drain well and dry thoroughly on kitchen paper.

Heat a wok until it is hot, add the oil and when it is almost smoking, add the chilli bean sauce or powder, garlic and black beans and stir-fry for about 30 seconds. Add the cucumber and toss well for about 3 seconds to coat in the spices. Add the stock and continue stir-frying over a high heat for 3–4 minutes, until almost all the liquid has evaporated and the cucumber is tender.

Transfer to a warmed serving dish. Sprinkle with the sesame oil, garnish with slices of raw cucumber and serve immediately.
Serves 4

ITALIAN BROAD BEANS

1.5 kg (3–3¹/₂ lb) small young broad beans (unshelled weight)
2 tablespoons olive oil
2 tablespoons chopped spring onions
1 slice rolled pancetta (see Note, below), 1 cm (¹/₂ inch) thick, cut into 5 mm (¹/₄ inch) strips
salt and pepper to taste
6 tablespoons chicken stock
1 tablespoon chopped parsley

Shell the broad beans and rinse in cold water.

Heat the oil in a wok and sauté the spring onions for 30 seconds. Add the pancetta and stir well. Add the broad beans and salt and pepper, toss well in the oil and pour over the stock. Cover and simmer for 6–8 minutes, until the beans are just tender. If there is any liquid left, remove the lid, increase the heat and boil rapidly, stirring constantly.

Transfer the beans to a warmed serving dish, sprinkle with the parsley and serve immediately.

Serves 4

Note: pancetta is the same cut of pork as bacon, which is cured in salt and spices. Usually available at Italian delicatessans and good grocers, it is sold tightly rolled in a salami shape. There is no exact substitute, but green bacon may be used instead.

ASPARAGUS AND MUSHROOMS

500 g (1 lb) asparagus
50 g (2 oz) butter
1 slice rolled pancetta (see Note, above) 1 cm (¹/₂ inch) thick, cut into 5 mm (¹/₄ inch) strips
250 g (8 oz) small button mushrooms
salt and pepper

Cut the asparagus into diagonal pieces, starting at the tip and working down towards the stem end. Use as much of the stem as is tender and discard the rest.

Melt the butter in a wok, add the asparagus and toss well. Cook, stirring, for 2 minutes, without browning.

Add the pancetta and mushrooms and cook for 5 minutes, until the vegetables are tender. Increase the heat and boil rapidly for 1 minutes, until all the liquid has evaporated. Season with salt and pepper and serve immediately.

Serves 4

RICE AND PASTA
CRISPY FRIED NOODLES

500 g (1 lb) egg noodles
salt
1 tablespoon vegetable oil
1 clove garlic, sliced
1 × 2.5 cm (1 inch) piece
  fresh root ginger, peeled
  and finely chopped
3 spring onions, chopped
125 g (4 oz) lean pork,
  sliced
125 g (4 oz) boned
  chicken breast, skinned
  and shredded
1 tablespoon soy sauce
1 tablespoon dry sherry
50 g (2 oz) frozen peeled
  prawns, thawed
3 celery sticks, sliced
  diagonally
125 g (4 oz) spinach,
  shredded

Cook the noodles in boiling salted
water until just tender; do not
overcook. Drain and rinse with cold
water.

Heat the oil in a wok, add the
garlic, ginger and spring onions and
stir-fry for 1 minute. Add the pork
and chicken and stir-fry for 2
minutes. Add the noodles and
remaining ingredients and cook for 3
minutes.

Pile on to a warmed serving dish
and serve immediately.
Serves 4–6

NOODLES TOSSED WITH MEAT AND VEGETABLES

2 tablespoons vegetable oil
2 green chillies, seeded
  and thinly sliced
1 clove garlic, thinly sliced
350 g (12 oz) minced pork
4 spring onions, sliced
1 small green pepper,
  cored, seeded and sliced
2 carrots, cut into
  matchsticks
3 celery sticks, cut into
  matchsticks
1/2 cucumber, cut into
  matchsticks
1 tablespoon soy sauce
2 tablespoons sweet red
  bean paste★
1 tablespoon dry sherry
350 g (12 oz) noodles,
  cooked

Heat the oil in a wok, add the chillies
and garlic and fry quickly for about
30 seconds. Add the pork and cook
for 2 minutes. Increase the heat, add
the vegetables and cook for 1 minute.
Stir in the soy sauce, bean paste,
sherry and noodles. Stir well to mix
and heat thoroughly.
    Pile on to a warmed serving dish
and serve immediately.
Serves 4–6

NOODLES IN SOUP

- 250 g (8 oz) peeled prawns
- salt
- 1 teaspoon cornflour
- 1 tablespoon cold water
- 350 g (12 oz) egg noodles or spaghettini
- 600 ml (1 pint) well-flavoured chicken stock
- 2 tablespoons light soy sauce
- 3 tablespoons vegetable oil
- 2 spring onions, thinly shredded
- 125 g (4 oz) bamboo shoots or button mushrooms, shredded
- 125 g (4 oz) spinach leaves, Chinese leaves or Cos lettuce, shredded
- 2 tablespoons Chinese rice wine, or dry sherry
- 1–2 teaspoons sesame oil, to finish (optional)

Place the prawns in a bowl with a pinch of salt. Mix the cornflour to a smooth paste with the cold water, then stir into the prawns.

Cook the noodles or spaghettini in a large saucepan of boiling salted water, then drain and place in a warmed large serving bowl or 4 individual bowls. Bring the stock to the boil and pour over the cooked noodles, with about half of the soy sauce. Keep hot.

Heat the oil in a hot wok, add the shredded spring onions to flavour the oil, then add the prawn mixture and the shredded vegetables. Stir a few times, add 1 1/2 teaspoons salt, the remaining soy sauce and the rice wine or sherry. Cook for about 1–2 minutes, stirring constantly. Pour the mixture over the noodles and sprinkle with the sesame oil if using. Serve the soup hot.

Serves 4